THE CIVIL RIGHTS MOVEMENT IN AMERICA

The
Civil Rights Movement
in America

Essays by
DAVID LEVERING LEWIS
CLAYBORNE CARSON
NANCY J. WEISS
JOHN DITTMER
CHARLES V. HAMILTON
WILLIAM H. CHAFE

Edited by
CHARLES W. EAGLES

UNIVERSITY PRESS OF MISSISSIPPI
Jackson and London

This volume has been sponsored by the
CENTER FOR THE STUDY OF SOUTHERN CULTURE
at the University of Mississippi.

The paper in this book meets the guidelines for permanence and
durability of the Committee on Production Guidelines for Book Lon-
gevity of the Council on Library Resources.

93   92   91   90   6   5   4   3

Library of Congress Cataloging-in-Publication Data

The Civil rights movement in America.

Bibliography: p.
Includes index.
1. Afro-Americans—Civil rights.   2. United States—
Race relations.   I. Lewis, David L.   II. Eagles,
Charles W.
E185.615.C585   1986   323.1′196073   86-5665
ISBN 0-87805-297-6 (alk. paper)
ISBN 0-87805-298-4 (pbk. : alk. paper)

Contents

Acknowledgments

The symposium on the civil Rights Movement took place at the University of Mississippi on October 2–4, 1985, under the sponsorship of the Department of History and the Center for the Study of Southern Culture. A number of individuals who contributed their time and effort warrant special recognition.

Dr. Cora Norman and the Mississippi Committee for the Humanities provided essential financial support. Their continuing interest in and assistance to the symposium series are greatly appreciated. Similarly, the National Endowment for the Humanities gave a crucial grant through its Division of Research Programs.

Without the conscientious efforts of the participants, the symposium could not have succeeded. Their contributions equalled the high standards evident in their own scholarship; moreover, the papers and commentaries sparked considerable discussion.

Chancellor R. Gerald Turner and Vice Chancellor Morris L. Marx were kind to address briefly the evening sessions of the symposium, and former Chancellor Porter L. Fortune, Jr., demonstrated his enduring interest by attending a number of sessions. The Department of History and the Southern Center are grateful for their support of the symposium.

Charles R. Wilson, director of the previous symposium, was a constant source of information and good advice; and Frederick E. Laurenzo, chairman of the Department of History, answered many questions, solved numerous problems, and handled innumerable last minute details. Sheila Skemp and Harry P. Owens helped at a particularly difficult time, and James J. Cooke did a fine job with what has become his annual duty. The departmental secretary, Susan Pettis, and her student assistant, Amanda Cook, worked with their usual skill, dispatch, and cheerfulness. At the

Southern Center, Martha Doyel and Sarah Dixon assisted with
many administrative problems. Ann J. Abadie, along with Mary
Betsy Bellande of the University Development Office, helped
with the submission of grant proposals.

The person indispensable for the success of the symposium was
my wife, Brenda. Her ideas and enthusiasm, her confidence and
support made it possible. Our son, Daniel, met the participants
and attended several sessions, even though he could not have
understood their significance. More important, he had a good
time and added to the enjoyment of others, especially his parents.

Introduction

Twenty-three years after James Meredith enrolled at the University of Mississippi, eleven noted scholars came to the University to discuss, examine, and analyze the Civil Rights Movement. Representing the disciplines of history, political science, and the law, they participated in the eleventh annual Chancellor's Symposium on Southern History. Their papers and the commentaries on them contribute to a clearer perception of what caused and motivated the Civil Rights Movement, how it functioned, the changes that occurred within it, and its accomplishments and shortcomings.

The Civil Rights Movement warrants such extensive examination because it had a profound effect on the modern South and the entire nation. From the United States Supreme Court's decision in *Brown v. Board of Education* in 1954 to the death of Martin Luther King, Jr., in 1968 and the waning of the movement in the late 1960s and early 1970s, blacks and whites engaged in a monumental struggle for black equality. The movement, of course, had antecedents to the *Brown* decision and has involved significant work since the 1960s, but the most important changes in racial segregation and discrimination occurred in the intervening decade and a half. Though the Civil Rights Movement did not solve what Gunnar Myrdal termed the "American dilemma," it did alter the status of blacks in southern society; it so changed relations between the races that C. Vann Woodward has called it the "second reconstruction."

Many Americans, but perhaps especially southerners, can certainly remember events and people from the days of the Civil Rights Movement, but their understanding of the movement remains in most cases limited to their own recollections of news accounts, their observations in their own local communities, and stories they have since heard about the movement. For many others, particularly the young, the Civil Rights Movement is not a memory but history, and they know little about it. Only in the last decade have scholars begun to study the Civil Rights Movement intensively and to provide the basis for a greater understanding of it.

The following six essays and the commentaries do not provide a comprehensive history of the Civil Rights Movement but instead analyze a few important aspects of it ranging from the movement's leadership to the movement in a single significant state. The authors are all scholars who have made outstanding contributions to the study of the movement.

The opening essay by David Levering Lewis seeks to explain the sources of the movement by boldly suggesting that "political demographics may truly be said to be racial destiny." In a cogent review of events from the 1930s to the early 1950s, he emphasizes the migration of blacks from the South to the urban North as a prerequisite for the movement. No commentary follows Lewis's paper because illness prevented the appearance of both the scheduled commentator and a substitute. Comments from the audience, however, proposed that Lewis paid insufficient attention to changes occurring within the South among blacks who remained in the region. He had, several indicated, neglected the indigenous southern origins of the movement.

In the second paper, Clayborne Carson also stresses the need to study the mass activism in hundreds of local communities. He calls for shifting the focus of inquiry from the large organizations, "professional reformers . . . and politicians" of a "national" civil rights movement to the "black freedom struggle" growing out of a myriad of issues at the local level. Questioning the importance of "institutionalized strategies and tactics" and the leaders who tried to implement them, Carson argues that local efforts frequently transformed "the structures that created them." In his commentary, Steven F. Lawson acknowledges the current imbalance in studying national organizations, leaders, and activities, and he predicts a new synthesis will recognize the intersection of and the "mutual relationship between strategies, tactics, goals, and ideologies nationally and locally," without neglecting either.

Even among the movement's leadership, however, Nancy J. Weiss finds disunity, competition, and tension, as well as cooperation. In the third essay, she contends that the pre-1965, direct-action phase of the movement was distinctive in its "simultaneous mobilization of diverse leadership working by different means toward a common goal." According to Weiss, who is working on a biography of Whitney Young of the National Urban League, the tensions were "creative" and the competition "salutary, indeed essential." David J. Garrow in his comments warns against minimizing the negative effects of the internal divisions, and he asks for a definition of leadership that includes more than "organizational chieftains or spokespersons."

The fourth essay examines leadership at the state level, as John Dittmer analyzes the internal politics of the Mississippi movement from 1954 to 1964. Drawing on his nearly completed study of the Civil Rights Movement in Mississippi, he finds significant changes occurring with the Freedom Rides in 1961 and after the 1964 Democratic national convention. Neil R. McMillen applauds Dittmer's periodization of the movement and his attention to class conflict in it, and he eagerly awaits fuller explication in Dittmer's book-length work.

The role of the federal law and courts in the Civil Rights Movement receives recognition from Charles V. Hamilton. He declares that the movement successfully ended *de jure* segregation by wisely following a legal attack. The courts, and especially the Supreme Court, were the "critical focal points" involved in that victory, according to Hamilton. In his comments, Mark V. Tushnet, who is studying the NAACP's legal strategy in fighting school segregation, demurs. He suggests instead that the courts were not unusually supportive and that the federal legal response was a collaboration among the courts, the congress, and the executive.

William H. Chafe in the final essay considers the results of the movement. He agrees with Hamilton that it won basic legal rights for the individual but finds that insufficient. Pointing to continuing discrimination involving gender, class, and race, Chafe calls for a new movement for collective action to provide equality of result for all, not just equality of opportunity for individuals. In his commentary, J. Mills Thornton, who is at work on a history of the Montgomery bus boycott, proposes that a shift from individualist to collectivist goals·helped kill the Civil Rights Movement in the late 1960s because collectivism violated traditional American values of personal liberty. He suggests that Chafe's call for a new collectivist movement is similarly "doomed inevitably to failure by the entire weight of American history."

While the speakers and commentators disagreed among themselves on many points, none argued that the Civil Rights Movement had insured equality and had eliminated racism and discrimination from American society. Clayborne Carson, for example, prefers the term "black freedom struggle" because it signifies that the movement was for more than civil rights, while Charles V. Hamilton points beyond what he sees as the successful quest for legal rights to a more difficult campaign for resources. John Dittmer ends his paper by mentioning the need for a "'Third Reconstruction' . . . /to/ address the ongoing problems of poverty and powerlessness." By deepening understanding of the Civil Rights Movement, the following essays may in some way contribute to efforts to solve American society's continuing problems.

C.W.E.

THE CIVIL RIGHTS MOVEMENT IN AMERICA

The Origins and Causes of the Civil Rights Movement

DAVID LEVERING LEWIS

If it is venturesome to suppose that anything analytically new may be offered as to the origins and causes of the Civil Rights Movement of the 1960s, it is equally true that the demography of this phenomenon is fundamental to its deepest comprehension. In this case, political demographics may truly be said to be racial destiny. In the two decades immediately following the outbreak of World War Two, almost three times as many Afro-Americans departed the South as had left during the Great Migration of the century's second decade—with 1,599,000 moving mostly North during the period 1940–1950, and 1,473,000 during the next ten years. The decade of the Sixties saw continued high migration, with some 1,380,000 more southern Afro-Americans outmigrating.

The political implications of this huge population shift were apparent to astute political observers as early as the 1928 presidential election, when the normally "solid" South divided its support between Herbert Hoover and Alfred E. Smith. For some Democrats, winning Afro-American voters in the urban North and East was seen as vital to garnering sufficient electoral votes to upset Hoover. Smith's campaign manager, the resourceful Mrs. Belle Moskovitz, persuaded him to offer the young assistant executive secretary of the National Association for the Advancement of Colored People (NAACP), Walter White, direction of the Smith-for-President Colored League. White and the NAACP leadership were assured that the Democratic standard bearer would adopt, publicly, a rhetoric of racial tolerance and, privately, a policy of seeking the counsel of and making federal appointments from the ranks of the civil rights establishment. Ultimately, white southern pressures forced Smith to renege. Walter White regretfully declined.[1] Nevertheless, about 20 percent of the Afro-American electorate voted for the Democrats, eight percent more than in previous elections.

Robert L. Vann, publisher of the Pittsburgh *Courier*, predicted that millions of his people would turn "the pictures of Abraham Lincoln to the wall" in the 1932 presidential election. With the unique exception, however, of Democratic Harlem, an even greater percentage voted for Hoover than before. What Walter White called the Afro-American's "chronic Republicanism" seemed fully reconfirmed with the rejection of Franklin D. Roosevelt. In fact, this was the last act in a drama of hidden attitudinal and political developments. The racial realignment was to come in the congressional elections two years later, when FDR's party won a majority of Afro-American voters for the first time in history. Howard University political philosopher Kelly Miller's pronouncement that the "Negro is no longer the wheelhorse of the Republican Party" fulfilled Robert Vann's prediction.

By 1936, the strategy pursued under Hoover to turn the southern GOP "lily white" was as dead as Prohibition—not to return until the Eisenhower Fifties. Alfred M. Landon wrapped himself in the mantle of Lincoln and Frederick Douglass, and Republicans inserted a fine-sounding civil rights plank in the national platform that year. Big city Democratic machines— Tammany in New York, Kelly-Nash in Chicago, Dickmann in St. Louis, Pendergast in Kansas City—lavished patronage on the black community. As Nancy Weiss shows, the Party effectively reminded Afro-Americans how well they had fared under FDR, after the misery caused by Hoover. "Let Jesus lead you, and Roosevelt feed you!" one popular slogan exhorted.[2]

Pat Watters and Reese Cleghorn observed of the years after

1934, "It was in this period that Negro votes and public policy at the presidential level became, in significant degree, cause and effect."[3] Northward migration reinforced the labor-urban-based wing of the Democratic Party, the wing in sympathy with the broader economic and social objectives of the New Deal. Southern Democrats in senior congressional positions not only meant disenfranchisement and segregation for Afro-Americans, but legislative obstructionism in the service of economic conservatism and regional parochialism. These were the Party satraps whom FDR finally publicly denounced as "feudal oligarchs" (Ellison Smith of South Carolina, Walter George of Georgia, Millard Tydings of Maryland, Martin Dies of Texas, Theodore Bilbo of Mississippi) and appealed directly but altogether unsuccessfully to their constituents to unseat some of them in the 1938 congressional elections. In matters of maximum importance to it, the South remained well in control of partisan and even national politics, but the emergence of countervailing forces within the Democratic Party was unmistakable.

As one of the key elements in this new coalition of power, Afro-Americans did, in fact, increase their advantages during the so-called Second New Deal (1936–1940). The new, more responsive Attorney General created the civil rights section in the Justice Department; the Department of Interior imposed racial quotas on WPA contractors; the Civilian Conservation Corps augmented Afro-American enrollment from 6 to 11 percent; other alphabet agencies recruited some 100 of the best and brightest Afro-American university graduates as midlevel bureaucrats (Ralph Bunche, William Hastie, Rayford Logan, et al.); finally, somewhat assuaging Afro-American anguish about his waffling over poll tax repeal and public silence about federal antilynching legislation, FDR delivered at Howard University his symbolic "no forgotten men and no forgotten races" speech. In 1940, the Democratic platform addressed itself directly for the first time to equal protection under law and due process rights for Afro-Americans.

By then, 48 percent of the Afro-American population was urban; and, although only about 23 percent of it resided outside the South, its concentration in key northern cities was imposing—13 percent of Philadelphia's total population; 13.5 percent of Detroit's; 13 percent of Indianapolis's; 8.3 percent of Chicago's (for a total of nearly 300,000); and 6.4 percent of New York's (477,000, a treble increase over the 1920 census). *Time* magazine had noted four years previously, if erroneously, "In no national election since 1860 have politicians been so Negro-minded as in 1936."[4] More significantly, in 1941, Ralph Bunche's *Journal of Negro Education* article, "A Critical Analysis of the Tactical Programs of Minority Groups," gave preliminary formulation to the crucial "balance of power" concept, to which NAACP publicist Henry Lee Moon devoted booklength treatment seven years later, and by which more than a generation of Afro-American policymakers and politicians have since been guided (sometimes overambitiously).[5]

Although isolation of any single election factor risks presenting a false picture, the reality that Afro-American votes were now potentially determinative in 16 non-South states with 278 electoral votes escaped no serious political strategist.[6] Thus, in the 1944 FDR-Dewey contest, Thomas E. Dewey would unquestionably have won if his percentage of Afro-American votes had been equivalent to Hoover's in 1932. Thus, once again, as at its historic 1936 national convention, the Democratic Party's presidential decisionmakers successfully calculated the risks of offending the South with Hubert Humphrey's strong 1948 civil rights plank. Four southern states went Dixiecrat, while Harry S. Truman narrowly defeated Dewey because, as historians August Meier and Elliott Rudwick state, 1948 was "the first election since Reconstruction in which the Negro's status was a major issue and in which his political power was a critical factor in the outcome."[7] Nevertheless, massive Afro-American support for Adlai Stevenson was irrelevant to the outcome four years later—a perfect object lesson in the limitations of the balance of power paradigm. Under Dwight D. Eisenhower, the Hoover strategy of winning the lily white South was again regnant. This devastating limitation aside—and it is the one by which Afro-Americans are currently bedeviled—"there had been," as Watters and Cleghorn affirm, "a revolution in the power to obtain results."[8]

A reductionist interpretation of postwar liberalism both distorts and disserves the considerable reserve of moral and constitutional principles by which that liberalism was powered. Fascism's doctrinal depravity, the solidarism of the war effort, and the trauma of the Holocaust deeply affected the collective American mind. There were not a few white southerners, and probably a majority of white northerners, who would have wished to say to the first sit-in students, as did the woman in the Greensboro Woolworth's, "you should have done this ten years ago."[9] George Fredrickson's *White Supremacy* has masterfully shown the potential for political and social inclusion of racial minorities that a constitutional commitment to egalitarian democracy can sustain and mobilize, even in the face of its longstanding nullification by formal and informal arrangements and compromises.[10] The official creeds of societies matter a great deal.

That said, it would be equally imperceptive to downplay the high degree of correspondence between the Afro-American's urbanization and outmigration from the South and the postwar mentality of racial meliorism. By 1950, the "power to obtain results" of Afro-Americans was running dangerously far ahead of the South's intellectual and institutional power to react constructively. Simultaneously, the racial attitudes in much of the rest of the nation were being transformed by that same potential power. Even the most casual reference to Tocqueville or Crane Brinton must have indicated a situation in which rising expectations and very slow social change presented the classic formula for upheaval, if not revolution—those flashpoint conjunctions which Ted Robert Gurr's work usefully assembles for our retrospective examination.[11] Was it not significant in this regard that the Carnegie Foundation, which had financed the massive study of another evolving racial crisis (that arising from unrest among South Africa's Afrikaner poor), produced, through Gunnar Myrdal and his regiment of social scientists, the ultimate liberal conceptualization of and prescription for the American dilemma?[12]

The impact of *An American Dilemma* was so potent that it controlled racial thought and policy for at least a decade. For all its impressive sociological panoply and perdurable insights, the Myrdalian analysis was imbedded in Hegelian idealism. Right ideas would gradually transform wrong institutions; the American Creed would ultimately reify itself because the compounding tensions between high ideals and ignoble realities would compel white Americans to reexamine the racial status quo. "The moral dilemma of the American [is] the conflict between his moral valuations on various levels of consciousness and generality," Myrdal writes.[13] If, as I believe, Stanford Lyman's contention is correct that the "entire body of Myrdal's argument is open to question" because of the explicit assumption that "'higher values' generally win out in the long run over 'lower' ones," all this matters rather less than the transformative power that *An American Dilemma* attained principally by legitimizing debate about the dilemma.[14]

Its publication came in the same year as the Supreme Court, after a twelve-year toleration of the fiction that southern white primaries were privately organized occasions, found its rare Fifteenth Amendment voice in *Smith v. Allwright*, definitively striking down this major franchise impediment. Two years later, came the presidentially impanelled Committee on Civil Rights, whose eloquent, comprehensive report was ready for publication in late 1947. *To Secure These Rights* spoke in Myrdalese of the moral imperatives of the American Creed, but it introduced a significant new reason for its fulfillment: "The United States is not so strong, the final triumph of the democratic ideal is not so inevitable that we can ignore what the world thinks of us or our record."[15] Another blue-ribbon, presidential committee produced, in time for the 1948 election, a searing expose of the social consequences of segregated education and a recommendation that all forms of educational segregation end as soon as possible. Finally, Harry Truman gave Afro-Americans the long-awaited presidential rhetoric, calling on Congress in his State of the Union message to enact significant civil rights legislation.

In all of these developments there was the resonance of political demography; but neither the reality nor the prospect of Afro-American votes counting heavily in close elections would have sufficed alone to produce the civil rights advances ahead. By the early Fifties, demographics had also yielded impressive economic benefits. Despite severe employment dislocation caused by temporary dismantlement of defense industries and two punishing recessions in 1953–54 and 1957–58, Afro-Americans generally prospered in the score of years after the War. During the period 1947 to 1974, according to the U.S. Census Bureau's global study, "the median income of Black families more than doubled," rising from 51 to 62 percent of white family income, with 51 percent becoming white collar.[16] During the late 1940's and early 1950's, the black unemployment rate of less than 2 percent was at its lowest relative to the white rate (which it otherwise tends to double).[17] *Jet* and *Ebony*, and a number of mainstream popular magazines, ballyhooed the new black purchasing power, calculated to be larger than the gross national product of several European nations.

Rising incomes also meant a tripling of the college population, with prewar Afro-American invisibility at northern white universities giving way to dramatic increase.[18] Predictably, there was now a steady supply of "exemplary" Afro-Americans (athlete Jackie Robinson joining the Dodgers in 1947, poet Gwendolyn Brooks winning a Pulitzer and jurist William Hastie appointed to a federal judgeship in 1949, diplomat Ralph Bunche receiving the Nobel Peace Prize in 1950)—racial paragons whose lives rebutted inferiority stereotypes, on the one hand, and, on the other, diverted attention from the distressing Marxism of W.E.B. Du Bois, Paul Robeson, and Benjamin Davis, Jr. Thus, in the Myrdalian decade after 1944, that article of faith of such civil rights leaders as James Weldon Johnson, Charles S. Johnson, and Walter White that the race problem was essentially not so much institutional or even economic but, rather, a phenomenon of collective psychology, now seemed verified.[19] Many white and black civil libertarians began to believe that those rhetorical taboos—usually beginning, "Would you want your daughter. . . ?"—might now be answered affirmatively, if the subject were Ralph Bunche, Jr., or Jackie Robinson, Jr.

In the case of the Supreme Court, the two taboo questions concerned housing and education. Richard Bardolph and Richard Kluger have amply documented the granite conservatism and infinite civil rights evasions of the Court during the administrations of FDR and Truman.[20] But New Deal and Fair Deal ideologies, reinforced by the Afro-American's increasingly credible political and economic presence, began the slow reversal of *Plessy v. Ferguson* in the late 1930's. The NAACP litigation strategy, conceived in 1931 during Nathan Margold's brief tenure as the first salaried legal counsel, produced, under Charles Hamilton Houston's inspired direction, a trickle and then a stream of Supreme Court victories. Beginning with *Missouri ex rel Gaines v. Canada*, the 1938 decision requiring University of Missouri Law School either to admit a single qualified applicant or build him a law school, continuing with the 1947 *Sweatt v. Painter* and 1948 *Sipuel v. Oklahoma* decisions, and climaxing with *McLaurin v. Oklahoma State Regents* in 1950, mandating truly equal professional school facilities, NAACP Lawyers had almost achieved their goal of making separate-but-equal higher education too expensive for the South.[21] In *McLaurin*, Chief Justice Fred M. Vinson's opinion had gone so far as to speculate on the possibility that separateness might be incompatible with equality. That same year, the NAACP filed its first public school segregation case before Judge J. Waties Waring of Charleston, South Carolina, contesting the educational policies in Clarendon County.

From one perspective, NAACP tactics simply made a virtue of

necessity: litigation focusing on higher education raised constitutional issues whose validation involved, as a practical matter, only a finite cohort of Afro-Americans. From another perspective—that of class interests—the NAACP's tactics, as well as those of the National Urban League and other major civil rights organizations, betrayed a consistent elitism. Martin Kilson reminds us that, until the mid-1960's, "civil rights politics was largely a middle-class affair, and the Negro lower strata had little political relationship to civil rights politics."[22] However finite the cohort, white, law, dental, and business school admissions were bread-and-butter exigencies to the civil rights establishment and its dues-paying supporters.

To be sure, quality public-school education was one of their paramount concerns, but, to a considerable extent, E. Franklin Frazier's black bourgeoisie had carved out tolerable enclaves for its children either in the urban public school systems of the South or through private means there.[23] Furthermore, for much of the Afro-American civil rights rank and file, there was a vested interest in separate equality in public school education (principalships, teaching positions, the two-income-per-family necessity). In this regard, it is worth a good Marxist speculation about the surprising fact revealed by Kluger that it was Judge Waring of South Carolina who persuaded Thurgood Marshall to withdraw and amend the NAACP's petition so as to challenge head-on the constitutionality of racial segregation.[24] There were good reasons why just plain folk called it the "National Association for the Advancement of *Certain* People."

It was this "certain people" syndrome that had caused the NAACP to be roundly criticized by many of the younger Afro-American intellectuals during the Du Bois-sponsored 1933 Amenia Conference—particularly the Association's hostility to organized labor and relative indifference to economic issues.[25] Here again, migration north generated an important alliance. So long as most Afro-Americans remained in the South (the majority of them as peasant farmers), locked into the Republican Party, they remained irrelevant to the concerns of organized labor. The shift to the Democrats made a labor-black alliance at least a possibility; although, with the important exception of A. Philip Randolph of the Brotherhood of Sleeping Car Porters, Afro-American leadership during much of the Thirties regarded organized labor as the prime enemy. As Herbert Hill has shown, the racial exclusivity of the AFL was endemic and chronic, "from Gompers to benign William Green to the current era of sophisticated public relations under George Meany. . . ."[26] But rampant mechanization of southern agriculture during the New Deal drove hundreds of thousands more unskilled Afro-Americans into northern industrial centers where fierce working-class white hostility to them as "scabs" was gradually attenuated, after the 1935 founding of the CIO, by a strategy of cooptation.

The collapse of such great labor strikes as Homestead in 1892 and the "Red Scare" steel strikes of 1919, as well as the 1927 United Mine Workers failure to organize the southern fields, was said to be attributable to black strike breakers.[27] With four out of five black workers unskilled, the Congress of Industrial Organization's John L. Lewis, Philip Murray, and David Dubinsky proclaimed the brotherhood of all and energetically set about organizing black coal miners, steel workers, and auto workers. The role of "SWOC" (the Steel Workers Organizing Committee) in cementing the new interracial alliance was crucial. SWOC funds flowed into the NAACP treasury, where they went to finance litigation and antilynch lobbying. In 1941, the longlived marriage of the NAACP and the United Automobile Workers occurred dramatically when patrician Walter White stood at the gate to Henry Ford's River Rouge plant with a bullhorn, exhorting black workers to join the union.[28] Weiss finds that CIO funds also struck a positive response from the deeply conservative National Urban League.[29]

While the American Federation of Labor remained as lily white as before, even its leadership soon found it useful to support rhetorically and financially the civil rights agenda, as well as to take such specific public relations steps as full admission of Randolph's Brotherhood of Sleeping Car Porters and official participation in Scottsboro and Angelo Herndon rallies.[30] Unskilled and skilled organized labor courted Afro-Americans for their own interests (interests largely coinciding with those of the Democratic Party), and Afro-Americans rallied to both from symmetrical motives. The very aggressive recruitment by communist unions of Afro-American membership and infiltration of Afro-American organizations, such as the National Negro Congress and Scottsboro defense groups, contributed a positive legacy of interracial activism. If, by 1940, the civil rights militancy of Harry Bridges's Marine Workers Industrial Union, Mike Quill's Transport Workers Union, and H. L. Mitchell's socialist-inspired Southern Tenant Farmers Union deadended in the debacle of the Popular Front, historians Harvard Sitkoff, Mark Naison, Nell Painter, Dan Carter, and Donald Grubbs *inter alia,* have shown how durably educative and energizing communist unionism could be.[31]

By the early 1950's, the cumulative impact of balance of power politics, rising incomes, federal court decisions, coalition with organized labor, and the string of exemplary racial "firsts," had primed much of the nation for an end to segregation. There was change even in the South, where *Smith v. Allwright* brought Afro-American registration from a mere 250,000 in 1944 to 1,008,614 by 1952—still only 20 percent of its voting age population there.[32] For a brief, incredible period, it seemed possible that gubernatorial politics might replicate Democratic presidential politics in Georgia and Alabama. In Georgia, former governor Ellis Arnall's protege, James Carmichael (candidate of urban, business, and progressive forces), polled more ballots than Eugene Talmadge in 1946, with the help of an overwhelming black vote—only to be denied office because of that state's infamous, rural-loaded "county unit" system.[33] In Alabama, populist Governor James Folsom opposed the Strom Thurmond Dixiecrats, courted "Nigra" votes, and stupefied white Alabamians with a

1949 Christmas message, declaring, "As long as the Negroes are held down by deprivation and lack of opportunity, all the other people will be held down alongside them."[34] Folsom's protege, George C. Wallace, later took the state in a different direction.

But Morton Sosna's "silent South" occasionally found its voice. Ralph McGill of the Atlanta *Constitution* and Virginius Dabney of the Richmond *Times-Dispatch*, while meticulously eschewing advocacy of racial integration, cautiously urged the abandonment of Jim Crow public transportation. The Chapel Hill sociologists, led by Howard W. Odum, and the Chapel Hill artists, influenced by Paul Green, expended much conscience-stricken passion, if not light, over the race problem. The Southern Regional Council, a gentlemanly, slightly interracial group of southern educators, debated, temporized, and finally, in 1951, authorized Arthur Fleming, its president, to state that it was "neither reasonable nor right that colored citizens of the United States should be subjected to the humiliation of being segregated by law." Of course, the loudest voice in the muted, Deep South was not a man's but Lillian Smith's whose novels and editorials in her *North Georgia Review* pricked the conscience of the white South. Fairly undetected, there were, as Aldon Morris's recent study reveals, highly significant civil rights developments occurring at the grass roots in numerous southern cities and towns. A new Afro-American leadership—ministerial and populist—was taking shape below the traditional oligarchic, white-black leadership configuration. Still, one had to have, as a reading of Sosna and Harry Ashmore indicates, the most restrained expectations for efficacious white southern liberalism in the 1950's.[35]

The stage was now set for decision in the five cases grouped as *Brown v. the Board of Education of Topeka, Kansas*. The sudden death of Chief Justice Vinson permitted the jurisprudentially radical reasoning—theories from sociology and psychology—leading to the Court's unanimous May 17, 1954 decision. In retrospect, the civil rights revolution appears to have been the inevitable consequence of *Brown*. "Revolution" here denotes social upheaval accompanied by collective citizen violence and extraordinary state intervention. Yet, at the risk of sinning counterfactually, it seems that the revolutionary character of civil rights might very well have been different—have been much more evolutionary—but for three interdependent factors. In order of ascending causal importance, those factors were: first, the internal politics of the Warren Supreme Court dictating, as the price of unanimity in *Brown*, a one-year stay of implementation and the enunciation of the anticlimactic, "all deliberate speed" doctrine; second, the collpase and supplanting of responsible southern white leadership in virtually every domain (religion, politics, business, education) by opportunists and extremists; and, third and decisively, the southern politics of the Eisenhower White House and the President's own race relations convictions.[36]

Eisenhower's well-known reactions—that Earl Warren's appointment had been a mistake and the decision foolish—and his refusal to endorse *Brown*, except in the negative sense of stating that it was law, was, as Ashmore, Kluger, Sitkoff, Anthony Lewis, and Steven Lawson among others have argued, calamitous.[37] It should be recalled that, for about two years after *Brown*, "all deliberate speed" meant just that in much of the South. About 700 of the 3000 southern school districts quietly desegregated, including, significantly, that of Hoxie township in rural Lawrence County, Arkansas. The governors of South Carolina and Virginia initially appealed for calm and promised dutiful compliance. "We will consider the matter and work toward a plan which will be acceptable to our citizens and in keeping with the edict of the Court," Virginia's governor promised.[38] If the white South was hardly enthusiastic about school desegregation and if, as the so-called 1956 Southern Manifesto attested, most of its leaders were plotting to retard implementation through legal casuistry and administrative procrastination, a course of outright white defiance and violence was probably not inevitable until Little Rock.

Here was the great political miscalculation. The Eisenhower

White House, with its eyes on 1956, had no intention of forfeiting a large, grateful southern white vote, despite its secret deal with Democrat Adam Clayton Powell to press for a civil rights act in exchange for the Harlem Congressman's endorsement of the President.[39] Ignorant of the South's cultural and political atavisms, White House evasions and silences were bound to produce the very no-holds-barred crisis they hoped to avoid. Laissez-faire that had worked with Senator Joseph McCarthy was mistaken. Some 530 cases of recorded violence and reprisals against southern Afro-Americans were recorded between 1955–1958. The 1955 Interstate Commerce Commission's order banning segregation in interstate travel had no writ in the Deep South. School integration was nonexistent in Virginia, Georgia, Alabama, Louisiana, Mississippi, and South Carolina. In eight Deep South states, 45,845 fewer Afro-Americans registered to vote between 1956 and 1958 because of intimidation.[40]

But a primary contribution of the white South to the civil rights revolution was its assault upon the NAACP. Texas and Alabama's injunctions, Georgia's annulment of tax exemption, Virginia's sedition acts, South Carolina's public employment prohibitions decimated the Association's chapters and made outlaws of the stalwarts. The Alabama NAACP could suppport Arthurine Lucy's successful admission to the University of Alabama; but it looked impotent when she was speciously expelled a few days later, while a local mob hooted. In this climate, Monroe County, North Carolina, NAACP chapter president Robert Williams, expelled by the national executive secretary for arming and drilling his members, was a predictable phenomenon. Little Rock, the South's 1957 redneck edition of Fort Sumter, was equally predictable. Scenting victory, Yale law professor Alexander Bickel wrote, "the southern leaders, or at least a sufficient number of them, sought to assure it by turning from litigation and agitation to direct action by the use of mobs."[41]

Meanwhile, Afro-American leadership was undergoing radical transformation. Southern Baptist preachers, conspicuous in the past for their civic parochialism and cautiousness, were leading desegregation boycotts—boycotts in which, for the first time, poor folk participated in large numbers. Audible above the din of demonstration was heard the baritone of a new leadership voice. "Give us the ballot," Martin Luther King, Jr., demanded from the Lincoln Memorial, during the May 1957 Prayer Pilgrimage to Washington:

> Give us the ballot and we will no longer have to worry the federal government about our rights. . . . Give us the ballot and we will get the people judges who love mercy. Give us the ballot and we will quietly, lawfully, and nonviolently, without rancor or bitterness, implement the May 17, 1954, decision of the Supreme Court.[42]

The students who listened to Martin Luther King concluded that what was not given would have to be taken.

Civil Rights Reform and the Black Freedom Struggle

CLAYBORNE CARSON

Social movements ultimately fail, at least in minds of many committed participants. As radicals and revolutionaries have discovered throughout history, even the most successful movements generate aspirations that cannot be fulfilled. Activists, particularly those in social movements that are driven by democratic ideals, often do not regard the achievement of political reform as conclusive evidence of success. Their activism drives them toward values that cannot be fully implemented except within the activist community. Thus, although American social movements provided a major impetus for the extension of civil rights to previously excluded groups, many abolitionists struggled for more radical transformation than was achieved through the Fourteenth and Fifteenth Amendments, and many feminists wanted more than the Nineteenth Amendment or the Equal Rights Amendment. Similarly, many black activists of the 1960s came to see themselves as seeking more than the civil rights acts of 1964 and 1965.

Because the emergent goals of American social movements have usually not been fulfilled, scholars have found it difficult to determine their political significance. Institutionalized political behavior rather than mass movements are the central focus of studies on American politics. Historians have portrayed social movements as important forces on behalf of reform but not as the decisive shapers of the reforms themselves. They typically devote little attention to the internal processes of social movements and view activists only as harbingers of change—colorful, politically impotent, socially isolated idealists and malcontents who play only fleeting roles in the drama of American political history.

Center stage is reserved for the realistic professional reformers who remain at the edges of movements and for politicians who respond to mass activism by channeling otherwise diffuse popular energies into effective reform strategies. Abolitionist activists, historians have suggested, did not free blacks from bondage through moral suasion or through other distinctive forms of anti-slavery militancy; instead, the Republican Party transformed abolitionist sentiments into a viable political program. Similarly, historians have noted that the initial Populist platform, itself a tepid manifestation of late-nineteenth century agrarian radicalism, was enacted by later generations of unradical reformers. Historians, in short, typically view social reform movements from a distance and see mass activism as significant only to the extent that it contributes to successful reform efforts using institutionalized strategies and tactics.

This view of mass activism reflects sociological approaches to the study of social movements that downplay their political functions. American sociologists of the 1950s and 1960s explained that social movements served to relieve widely shared discontents that resulted from strains in the social system. Implicit or explicit in most sociological studies of American social movements was the notion that they were more likely to serve psychological rather than instrumental functions, that they manifested inchoate, individual discontent rather than serious, even if unsuccessful, political strategies involving organized groups. Historians influenced by sociological studies of social movements have argued, for example, that the abolitionists were psychologically abnormal or that populists were reacting against the passing of a familiar agrarian society.

Until recent years, the classical sociological view of social movements prevailed in the study of what is generally called the civil rights movement. Use of the term "civil rights" itself is based on the assumption that the southern black movements of the 1960s remained within the ideological boundaries of previous civil rights activism. Many social scientists studying black protest participation insisted that activism resulted from a distinctive psychological state that was shared by activists. According to an extensive literature, based largely on survey data rather than field observation of ongoing struggles, protest participation was most likely among blacks who had become increasingly aware of the discrepancies, or dissonance, between their conditions of life and the alternatives made possible by the rapidly changing surrounding society. As one sociologist put it, black protesters were distinguished from other blacks by a "higher awareness of the wider society" which made them "more prone to develop the particular set of attitudes and perceptions that lead to protest."[1]

Social scientists found it much easier to offer such analyses of the black struggle during the first half of the 1960s, when there were few signs of dissension within the movement over integrationist goals. During the last half of the decade, however, it became increasingly difficult to explain black power militancy as the outgrowth of the frustrated integrationist desires of blacks. Nevertheless, the classical sociological perspective continued to dominate scholarly writings regarding black militancy. If mass black activism could not be understood as a somewhat unwieldy tactic for achieving longstanding civil rights objectives, it was still possible to portray it as a politically unproductive or even counterproductive expression of mass frustration. Few scholars have been willing to study the internal dynamics of black social movements or to examine their varied and constantly changing strategies, tactics, and styles of leadership. As the nonviolent struggles of the early 1960s gave way to the violent racial conflicts of the late 1960s, the understandable reluctance of scholars, most of whom were white, to study black movements close up rather than from afar became more and more evident.

Thus, until recently, the civil rights literature was comprised mainly of studies of the major national civil rights leaders and their organizations. Following the lead of sociologists, most historians assumed that the black insurgences of the decade after the Montgomery bus boycott could best be understood within the context of a national campaign for civil rights reform. They saw mass activism among blacks as an extension of previous institutionalized civil rights reform efforts. To be sure, historians recognized that the new activism went beyond the once dominant NAACP tactics of litigation, lobbying, and propagandizing, but they saw increased black activism as a new tactic within a familiar strategy based on appeals to power. Protest was a product of widespread black dissatisfaction with the pace of racial change rather than with underlying strategies to achieve change. Instead of viewing mass activism as an independent social force, with its own emergent values and ideology, scholars were more likely to see it as an amorphous source of social energy that could be directed by the leaders of national civil rights organizations.

Indeed, some historical accounts have stressed the decisive role of white politicians rather than civil rights leaders in guiding the effort to achieve civil rights reforms. Thus, Arthur M. Schlesinger's account of the Kennedy presidency illustrated a common theme in surveys of the 1960s when it described Kennedy as a leader seeking to "keep control over the demand for civil rights" through timely concessions which would "hold the confidence of the Negro community." In broader terms, Schlesinger portrays Kennedy as moving "to incorporate the Negro revolution into the democratic coalition and thereby [helping] it serve the future of American freedom."[2] More recently, Carl M. Brauer gave more attention to the black protest movement as an independent force for change, but he too concluded that Kennedy usually maintained the initiative, driven by his need "to feel that he was leading rather than being swept along by events." When black militancy threatened to get out of hand in the spring of 1963, Brauer recounts, the President "boldly reached out to grasp [the reins of leadership] once again."[3]

Studies of civil rights organizations and their leaders understandably give more emphasis to the role of these organizations and their leaders than do studies of presidential leadership, but nonetheless these writings are ambiguous regarding the extent to which organizations and leaders were able to mobilize and direct the course of black militancy. They have focused on the strategies developed by national civil rights groups, while portraying mass activism as a new instrument in the arsenal of national civil rights leaders. The result has been that we have many studies of national civil rights leaders, particularly Martin Luther King, Jr., but few that attempt to determine the extent to which civil rights leaders reflected the aspirations of participants in black struggles.

This failure to clarify the shifting relationship between leadership and mass struggle is a glaring deficiency of studies that imply that national civil rights organizations and leaders played decisive roles in mobilizing southern blacks as a force for change during the 1950s and 1960s. Although the scholarship of the last five years has begun to rectify this deficiency, the perspective of the previous civil rights literature continues to reflect as well as shape the prevailing popular conception of the black struggle.

Embedded in this literature is the assumption that the black struggle can best be understood as a protest movement, orchestrated by national leaders in order to achieve national civil rights legislation. As already noted, use of the term civil rights movement, rather than such alternatives as black freedom struggle, reflects the misleading assumption that the black insurgences of the 1950s and 1960s were part of a coordinated national campaign. Viewing the black struggle as a national civil rights reform effort rather than a locally-based social movement has caused scholars to see Birmingham in the spring of 1963 and Selma in the winter and spring of 1965 as the prototypical black protest movements of the decade. In reality, however, hundreds of southern communities were disrupted by sustained protest movements that lasted, in some cases, for years.

These local protest movements involved thousands of protesters, including large numbers of working class blacks, and local organizers who were more concerned with local issues, including employment opportunities and political power, than with achieving national legislation. Rather than remaining within the ideological confines of the integrationism or King's Christian-Gandhianism, the local movements displayed a wide range of ideologies and proto-ideologies, involving militant racial or class consciousness.[4] Self-reliant indigenous leaders who headed autonomous local protest organizations have been incorrectly portrayed as King's lieutenants or followers even when they adopted nonviolence as a political weapon rather than a philosophy of life and were clearly acting independently of King or of the Southern Christian Leadership Conference, which he headed.

At present, few detailed studies of these sustained local movements have appeared, but William Chafe's study of Greensboro and Robert J. Norrell's study of the Tuskegee black movement, to cite two examples, reveal that local black movements were unique and developed independently of the national civil rights organizations.[5] Blacks in these communities developed their own goals and strategies which bore little relation to national campaigns for civil rights legislation. King was the pre-eminent national black leader, the exemplar of Gandhian ideals, but in Greensboro, Tuskegee, and many other communities, local leaders and organizers played dominant roles in mobilizing blacks and articulating the emergent values of the local struggles.

Careful examinations of local movements, therefore, challenge the assumption that national leaders, notably Martin Luther King, orchestrated local protest movements in their efforts to alter national public opinion and national policy. There is much to suggest that national civil rights organizations and their leaders played only minor roles in bringing about most local insurgences. It was more often the case that local black movements produced their own distinctive ideas and indigenous leadership rather than that these movements resulted from initiative of national leaders.

The Montgomery bus boycott, for example, began in 1955 as

the result of an unplanned act of defiance by Rosa Parks. Martin Luther King, Jr., emerged as a spokesman and as a nationally-known proponent of nonviolent resistance only after Montgomery blacks had launched their movement and formed their own local organization—the Montgomery Improvement Association. King's organization, the Southern Christian Leadership Conference, was formed only after the boycott ended. To be sure, the Montgomery struggle was an extension of previous civil rights reform efforts, but it began as an outgrowth of local institutional networks rather than as a project of any national civil rights organization.[6]

Similarly, no national organization or leader initiated the next major stage of the black struggle, the lunch counter sit-ins of 1960. SCLC, CORE, and the NAACP attempted to provide ideological and tactical guidance for student protesters after the initial sit-in in Greensboro, but student activists insisted on forming their own local groups under student leadership. Even the Student Nonviolent Coordinating Committee, which was founded by student protest leaders, was unable to guide the sit-in movement—a fact that contributed to SNCC's subsequent support for the principle of local autonomy.[7]

CORE initiated the Freedom Rides of 1961, but this desegregation effort did not become a major social movement until CORE abandoned the rides after protesters were attacked by whites in Alabama. Student militants formed their own organizations. Hundreds of student freedom riders then brought the movement into Mississippi and later to other parts of the South.[8]

The Freedom Rides provided a stimulus for the massive Albany protests of December 1961, which became a model for mass mobilizations of black communities elsewhere in the South. Each of the national civil rights organizations tried to offer guidance for the mass marches and demonstrations which culminated in the Birmingham protests of spring 1963, but by the summer of that year it had become clear to national black leaders that the black struggle had acquired a momentum over which they had little control. A. Philip Randolph, the black leader who proposed a march on Washington, told President Kennedy, "The Negroes are already in the streets. It is very likely impossible to get them off. If they are bound to be in the streets in any case, is it not better that they be led by organizations dedicated to civil rights and disciplined by struggle rather than to leave them to other leaders who care neither about civil rights nor about nonviolence?"[9] Malcolm X recognized and identified with the local black leadership that mobilized the black insurgences of 1963: "In Cambridge, Maryland, Gloria Richardson; in Danville, Virginia, and other parts of the country, local leaders began to stir up our people at the grass-roots level. This was never done by these Negroes of national stature."[10]

Even this brief discussion of the early history of the southern black struggle should reveal a major weakness of studies that assumed that King played a dominant initiating role in southern protests. These studies have not determined the extent to which King was actually able to implement his nonviolent strategy in specific places. Studies focused on civil rights leaders and organizations, rather than on local movements, often give the impression that King was not only the major national spokesman for the black struggle but also its prime instigator.

During the period from 1956 to 1961, however, King played only a minor role as a protest mobilizer as opposed to his role as a national symbol of the black struggle. Acknowledgement that King had limited control over the southern struggle should not detract from his historical importance as a heroic and intellectually seminal leader; recognition of King's actual role instead reminds us that his greatness was rooted in a momentous social movement. Numerous black communities organized bus boycotts and, later, sit-in movements with little direct involvement by King, who was seen by many black activists as a source of inspiration rather than of tactical direction. Even in Albany, where he played a major role in the 1961 and 1962 protests, he joined a movement that was already in progress and worked alongside indigenous leaders who often accepted but sometimes rejected his advice. In St. Augustine, Birmingham, and Selma, he also assisted movements that had existed before his arrival. In numerous other communities, movements arose and were sustained over long periods with little or no involvement by King or his organization.

Moreover, these local movements should not be viewed as protest activity designed to persuade and coerce the federal government to act on behalf of black civil rights. There was a constant tension between the national black leaders, who saw mass protest as an instrument for reform, and local leaders and organizers who were often more interested in building enduring local institutions rather than staging marches and rallies for a national audience. Local black leadership sought goals that were quite distinct from the national civil rights agenda. Even in communities where King played a major role, as in Albany, Birmingham, and Selma, he was compelled to work with local leaders who were reluctant, to say the least, to implement strategies developed by outsiders.

Black communities mobilized not merely to prod the federal government into action on behalf of blacks but to create new social identities for participants and for all Afro-Americans. The prevailing scholarly conception of the civil rights movement suggests a movement that ended in 1965, when one of the last major campaigns led by a civil rights organization prompted the passage of the Voting Rights Act. The notion of a black freedom struggle seeking a broad range of goals suggests, in contrast, that there was much continuity between the period before 1965 and the period after. Contrary to the oft-expressed view that the civil rights movement died during the mid-1960's, we find that many local activists stressed the continuity between the struggles to gain political rights for southern blacks and the struggles to exercise them in productive ways. Rather than claiming that a black power movement displaced the civil rights movement, they would argue that a black freedom movement seeking generalized racial advancement evolved into a black power movement toward the unachieved goals of the earlier movement.

In summary, scholars have portrayed the black struggle as an augmentation of traditional civil rights reform strategies directed by national civil rights organizations. They have stressed the extent to which national civil rights leaders were able to transform otherwise undirected mass discontent into an effective instrument to speed the pace of reform.

This conception of the black struggle has encountered a strong challenge from a new generation of scholars who have closely examined the internal dynamics of the black struggle in order to determine its sources and emergent norms. As suggested above, previous scholarly studies become increasingly deficient in explanatory power as scholars move nearer to the black struggle itself. If the black struggle were to be seen as a series of concentric circles, with liberal supporters on the outside and full-time activists at the center, the older scholarly literature would appear adequate in its description of dramatic, highly-publicized confrontations in Albany, Birmingham, and Selma and its treatment of the impact of these confrontations on public opinion and the national government. But the literature fails, for the most part, to explain what occurred at the core of the black struggle where deeply committed activisits sustained local movements and acquired distinctive tactics, strategies, leadership styles, and ideologies. It was among activists at the core of the struggle that new radical conceptions of American society and black identity emerged. The scholarly literature helps in explaining why a black person gained new rights, but this literature has been less successful in explaining why a black person is now likely to bring quite different attitudes to whatever he or she does than would have been the case before the black struggle began.

Among the recently published works that offer appealing new perspectives for viewing the black struggle as a social movement are the historical studies of specific local movements, such as

those of Chafe, Norrell, and those currently being written by
J. Mills Thornton on Montgomery and John Dittmer on Mississippi. These and other studies should provide a fuller understanding of the local context of the black struggle.

Several young sociologists have also charted some promising
new directions in the civil rights literature. Doug McAdam[11]
delivered the most sweeping assault yet on the theoretical under-
pinnings of the previous civil rights literature. He recognized that
this literature was rooted in inappropriate classical sociological
theories of social movements that focus attention on discontented
individuals seeking to manage the psychological strains associated with temporary disruptions of the social equilibrium. His
alternative perspective points to the political character of the
black struggle, which, he argues, arises not simply from increasing discontent, but from a growing recognition among discontented people that they have the power to alter their conditions of
life.

Yet, although McAdam's political process model can serve as a
useful way to examine the black struggle, his use of historical
evidence remains open to question. Rather than beginning with a
broad definition of indigenous organization among blacks, he
attempts to demonstrate the importance of indigenous organizations by pointing to the role played by the major civil rights
organizations in the black insurgences of the 1960's. After examining the *New York Times* index, he comes to the unsurprising
conclusion that most of the *Times'* reports mentioned the involvement of the major civil rights groups in protest activity. McAdam
should be troubled by the fact that the civil rights groups may
have influenced the news reporting by directing reporters' attention to activities in which the group was involved and that the
reporters themselves may have had difficulty assessing the nature
of organizational involvement in protest activity. The utility of
McAdam's model would have been even more convincingly demonstrated if he had recognized that political processes take

unique forms in each local context and that extensive research is needed to determine what roles particular types of national and local institutions play in a specific social movement.

Aldon Morris[12] offers a perspective similar in many respects to McAdam's, although he is more concerned with studying the social context of the black struggle than with carrying on a dialogue with previous civil rights scholarship. Morris makes an admirable attempt to do something that the previous generation of scholars neglected to do—that is, to determine how as well as why movements arise and to do this by actually undertaking serious historical research. His original interviews with many of the leaders of the black struggle are themselves wonderful contributions to historical scholarship. Just as McAdam's historical sources do not always serve his analytical purposes, however, so Morris's interviews provide an insufficient base on which to rest his argument.

On the one hand, Morris seeks to demonstrate that indigenous black institutional and leadership networks played major roles in sustaining the black struggle; this is a notion I have no difficulty accepting. On the other hand, he also wants to show that pre-existing black institutions invariably initiated and sustained those struggles. His evidence demonstrates that these organizations provided vital resources for those individuals who initiated the local movements, but far more careful research into documentary evidence from the period would be needed to assess the role played by civil rights organizations as opposed to individuals acting independently of those organizations. In some instances, my own interviews with the same individuals placed greater emphasis on the restraining influence on black activism of pre-existing organizations. In numerous instances, isolated individuals engaged in protest-intiating actions that were unauthorized by any organization, and these voluntary actions served as catalysts for mobilizing existing institutions into action. To conclude, for example, that spontaneity played little role in the sit-ins of 1960s because many individuals involved in initiating the sit-ins were affiliated with organizations is to downplay the disruptive impact of the sit-ins on those organizations.

Both McAdam, because of his reliance upon newspaper sources, and Morris, because of his insufficient use of primary sources from the period under examination, do not give sufficient attention to the importance of institutional transformation as basic themes in local black struggles. While it is true that the national civil rights organizations played major roles in the southern struggle, it is also the case that these organizations operated in a constantly changing context to which they were forced to respond. Morris relies upon the useful concept of "local movement center" to describe the "dynamic form of social organization" that sustained the struggle, but, surprisingly, his use of the concept conveys little of the dynamism that actually made such centers sources of tactical and ideological innovation.

It should be possible to direct attention to the fact that pre-existing institutions, leaders, and organizations were critically involved in all phases of the struggle without losing sight of the numerous ways in which activism served to challenge existing arrangements in black communities. To maintain, for example, that existing black church networks were vital to the struggle should not lead us to ignore the fact that many black churches did little to aid the struggle, did not join the umbrella organizations that came into being to sustain protest activity, and often were unwilling even to allow civil rights meetings to take place inside their buildings. To maintain that pre-existing civil rights groups played crucial roles in the struggle should not lead us to conclude that they always did so without prodding from activists or without considerable internal policy conflicts. To maintain that many black protest leaders were already part of the leadership structure of black communities is to ignore the extent to which the sudden rise to prominence of a leader such a King disrupted existing patterns of leadership.

Despite these criticisms, McAdam, Morris, and the historians who have done careful study of local movements have offered us important insights which correct the still-dominant view that movements are typically peripheral to institutionalized structures and to the process of political change. But this insight needs to be combined with an understanding of the capacities of social movements to transform the structures that created them, to generate new ideas and values, and to transform the people who become involved in them. Careful study of the internal dynamics of the black struggle will make us more aware of the ways in which institutions of various types can sustain movements or can kill them. Studies of the historical black struggles of 1960's currently being conducted by the many talented scholars entering this exciting field might also suggest how the vastly greater resources of contemporary black communities might be mobilized to renew the struggle.

Commentary / Steven F. Lawson

Clay Carson has presented a very thoughtful paper challenging the basic historical conceptualization of the civil rights movement. His paper offers a useful corrective to the manner in which most scholars portray the civil rights movement. Indeed, Carson prefers to rename the movement the "black freedom struggle." The change in nomenclature is not merely a matter of semantics; rather, it alters how we conceive of what the movement against racism in this country was all about. It also raises questions about our understanding of the dynamics of social change. In short, does change occur from the top down within the framework of a pluralist system or does it generate from the bottom up through the engine of indigenous mass movements? Carson emphasizes the latter, and he exhorts his colleagues to study local protest movements to discover their own unique life styles, ideologies, strategies, and tactics. In fact, several recent monographs on Greensboro, Tuskegee, and St. Augustine have done just that and several other works in progress are taking this approach.

Those including this commentator, who have written about the work of major civil rights organizations, leaders, and the efforts to enact national legislation or win litigation are taken to task for holding three incorrect assumptions. Clay has shown good taste in omitting the names of the culprits. Professor Carson is not necessarily wrong, but that does not make him entirely right. To some degree, he is creating and then attacking a series of straw men. No one would dispute his assertions that Martin Luther King, Jr., and influential civil rights leaders built upon rather than initiated mass protest activities or that local protest movements often had independent agendas from those of national organizations. When it came to tactics such as sit-ins, bus boycotts, and to a lesser extent freedom rides, the initiative generally started from below and worked its way upward. There is still a lot more to learn about the extent to which this was true in diverse communities throughout the South and the extent to which local branches and affiliates of national organizations such as the NAACP provided the impetus.

Professor Carson is absolutely correct in his comments concerning the role of John F. Kennedy and Lyndon B. Johnson in the civil rights struggle. As national politicians, they did not create civil rights protest, as has sometimes been implied—they reacted to it. Scholars should not neglect investigating their responses, for they will tell us much about the nature of liberal reform and the relationship of presidential leadership to mass protest movements. It is not inappropriate to conclude that the occupants of the White House sought to channel the forces of social disruption into safe and moderate courses. In this direction they often enlisted the cooperation of established civil rights groups competing for power and prestige within the movement.

However many pieces of well-needed legislation Congress enacted during the 1950s and 1960s, they would have had little impact without the efforts of local civil rights groups in organizing their communities for black freedom. Not only did they provide the funds and personnel to confront the status quo, their activities created a culture supportive of liberation. Out of their sundry protest efforts emerged a black consciousness and solidarity that went beyond any specific goal they may have been seeking. Where civil rights groups operated, black people collectively assisted each other in reducing the level of fear that had reinforced white supremacy for generations. How local blacks perceived their goals and adopted strategies to obtain them remains to be explored more fully and precisely in the studies Professor Carson calls upon us to write. Scholars will also have to discover to what degree mass movements defined aims such as voting rights, fair employment practices, and desegregation of public facilities differently than did national civil rights groups and their political allies.

Once scholarly inquiry has countered the top-heavy inbalance in the current literature on the black liberation struggle, a new synthesis will be required to bring the issue of social change into sharper focus. This task should take into account the ways in which efforts in the national arena intersected with those at the grassroots level. In doing so, it may be necessary to revise Professor Carson's depiction of the freedom struggle as a collection of separate spheres with local black movements looking inward and national groups facing to the outside. While this image places mass movements in black communities at the center of protest activities where they belong, it does not acknowledge sufficiently the mutual relationship between strategies, tactics, goals, and ideologies nationally and locally. The federal government provided the legal superstructure for the attainment of civil rights, whereas indigenous black organizations furnished the network to build solidarity, awaken racial consciousness, and utilize the freedoms born from struggle. In this respect, we can follow up on Professor Carson's valuable suggestion for examining whether the civil rights movement survived the mid 1960s. "We find," he declares, "that many local activists stressed the continuity between struggles to gain political rights for southern blacks and the struggle to exercise them in productive ways."

The suffrage offers an excellent opportunity for exploring the nature of the interaction between federal involvement and local concerns. Enfranchisement was both a strategy and a tactic for emancipation. The acquisition of the right to vote presumably would provide the necessary tool to obtain a broad range of civil rights and to protect them once they were secured. There does not appear to be a contradiction between national civil rights groups and indigenous organizations on this point. Moreover, without the passage of the Voting Rights Act of 1965 and its three successive renewals, the exercise of the ballot would not have been a resource available to black activists and proponents of social change. At the same time, as black voters began using the franchise to improve their social and economic conditions, they helped reformulate the meaning of the Voting Rights Act. Rather than exclusively a right-to-register law, it was transformed into a code for assisting black communities in the election of candidates of their own race. This changing interpretation of the law emerged from the first-hand experiences of black people in local areas, but it was carefully nurtured by civil rights legislation and litigation forged in Congress and the courts and implemented by the executive branch. In this instance, national and local civil rights interests were mutually reinforcing.

Nevertheless, there were serious divisions in tactics and strategies over the suffrage. The debate between those who advocated coalitionist alliances with white liberals and organized labor and those who championed separatist political arrangements is a familiar one. In this case, as Professor Carson suggests, it will be most helpful to investigate closely how local black political organizers perceived their roles and the instrument of the ballot. They probably saw the vote not as an end in itself but as a means of gaining black empowerment. Not simply a tactic for achieving certain concrete economic benefits, it also allowed blacks to take a greater measure of control of their lives and reach decisions that reflected their own desires and aspirations and not those imposed upon them. There have been many successes and failures toward these ends, and it is important for local community studies to analyze the forces promoting and retarding change.

This analysis should include internal factors—the availability of economic resources, the adequacy of organizing skills, individual and group rivalries, and the residue of traditional racial patterns. Other factors are external. It is here that the need to pay close attention to the structural limitations placed on black empowerment by the established electoral, constitutional, and economic systems becomes apparent. Strategies and tactics of mass protest movements were shaped by such institutions as the federal system, the two party system, and the corporate capitalist economy that relegated a large segment of the black population to a permanent underclass. In addition, remedial legislation such as the Voting Rights Act has reinforced the manner in which blacks compete for power by putting a premium on electoral politics and traditional forms of political activities. However much black community organizers attacked the conditions of impoverishment and disfranchisement, they had to do so within this institutional framework that restricted the magnitude of change. They had to develop strategies and tactics reflecting the underlying reality that empowerment must occur in a society in which blacks remained numerical minority. Political power was more easily achieved on the municipal and county levels where blacks constituted a majority of the electorate, but such successes did not automatically yield the tangible economic benefits that could come from state and federal action.

In this context, black power and coalitionist strategies were both tried, and in practice the conflicts between the two were more apparent than real. The former developed in the South not from any national groups' ideological blueprint but from the daily experiences of people trying to mold their own political destiny. In rural black-belt counties in the South, black power arose directly from civil rights organizing and also from the unwillingness of local whites to join alliances with blacks. However, the experiences of the Mississippi Freedom Democratic Party and the National Democratic Party of Alabama, both of which succumbed to untimely deaths, suggest that independent third parties were not enough for black liberation. Without some sort of biracial coalition building among progressive groups, black political strength remained limited and confined to areas where the resources for material change were too narrow. Civil rights groups must again dedicate themselves to providing resources and volunteers to foster the process of community organizing that was prematurely abandoned in the late 1960s. The legacy of SNCC, CORE, and SCLC persists in the areas where their field staff worked, but their efforts were not extended far enough or deeply enough to many places where they were sorely needed.

For the sake of the future, scholars need to reexamine the past to derive new lessons for the ongoing freedom struggle. They should try to view national civil rights efforts aimed at legislation, litigation, and publicity and the community organizing for black liberation aimed at consciousness raising as part of the larger process of empowerment. In an interactive way, they might see how the movement transformed local black institutions and guided national goals as well as how the actions of the national government and established civil rights groups affected local communities. Clay Carson's advice presented here today should help students of the movement reach these insights more quickly.

Creative Tensions in the Leadership of the Civil Rights Movement

NANCY J. WEISS

One of the persistent themes in the increasingly rich literature on civil rights leadership is the debilitating effect on the movement of competition among organizations and individuals who sought to lead it. Throughout the direct action phase of the movement, the Student Nonviolent Coordinating Committee (SNCC), the Congress of Racial Equality (CORE), the Southern Christian Leadership Conference (SCLC), and the National Association for the Advancement of Colored People (NAACP) competed vigorously for publicity and position. The organizations jockeyed for headlines, elbowed one another out of the limelight, moved in on each other's demonstrations, and took issue with each other's tactics. At the same time, individuals coined disparaging labels to describe leaders with whom they disagreed.[1]

What was at stake in this competition and sniping was considerably more than vanity or prestige. Getting the credit for mobilizing demonstrators or negotiating change translated into tangible resources—more adherents, increased financial support, easier access to the white power structure—resources that were essential to a leader's ability to lead and to an organization's ability to survive and flourish.

There is no denying that this kind of competition had negative effects. When name-calling and disputes among the leaders became public knowledge, it proved demeaning and gave the movement's opponents significant political leverage. When, as was frequently the case at the local level, suspicion and conflict between organizations diverted time and energy to one-upping, containing, or negotiating with a rival group, it obviously became more difficult to make headway toward the larger goals of deseg-regation.

Still, the very diversity of leadership that bred competition also proved salutary, indeed essential, to the fortunes of the civil rights movement in its direct-action phase. The complexity of the movement's goals; the variety of publics, black and white, that it needed to mobilize; the range of laws, practices, and customs that needed to be altered; and the broad array of strategies and tactics required to accomplish large-scale social change all demanded the simultaneous enlistment of organizations and leaders who could attack the problem from different, sometimes competing perspectives. Thus the models sociologists posit to describe the leadership of social movements—charismatic, enthusiastic, agita-tional leadership giving way to bureaucratic; or cyclical alterna-tion between mobilizers and articulators—do not accurately capture the essence of the civil rights movement in its direct-action phase. What was distinctive about the civil rights move-ment up to 1965 was the simultaneous mobilization of diverse leadership working by different means toward a common goal. The movement needed charismatic leaders as well as bu-reaucrats, mobilizers as well as articulators.

Leaders and organizations in the civil rights movement cooper-ated at the same time that they competed. Sometimes they did so formally, creating new structures to facilitate their efforts toward common ends. Sometimes the cooperation emerged without ad-vance planning or formal organization, as different organizations contributed in their own ways to the accomplishment of a single, overriding goal. From time to time the virtues of diversity proved themselves not in cooperation, whether conscious or de facto, but in the ability to make creative use of competition, as leaders and organizations played deliberately on the differences among themselves as a tactic to move whites who would otherwise have been less receptive to demands for change.

Organized attempts at cooperation among a diverse group of leaders proved essential to the fortunes of the civil rights movement in local communities in the South. Aldon D. Morris has argued for the crucial role of new umbrella organizations (in his terms, "organization[s] of organizations"), embracing black churches, the NAACP, political organizations, and citizens' associations, in initiating and sustaining bus boycotts in Baton Rouge, Montgomery, and Tallahassee in the 1950s, as well as a direct-action protest against discrimination in hiring, bus and train segregation, school segregation, and segregation in places of public accommodation in Birmingham in 1956. These new protest organizations—the United Defense League in Baton Rouge, the Montgomery Improvement Association, the Tallahassee Inter Civic Council, and the Alabama Christian Movement for Human Rights—stimulated the organization of "local movement centers" throughout the South in the late 1950s. In Nashville, Petersburg, Shreveport, and other cities, movement centers, with "interrelated set[s] of protest leaders, organizations, and followers," devised tactics and strategies, trained demonstrators, and launched direct-action protests to attain collectively-defined goals. What gave these movement centers their special character and their ability to sustain organized social protest was their incorporation in a common effort of a range of "direct action organizations of varied complexity."[2]

At the national level, organized attempts at formal cooperation among civil rights leaders and organizations were short-lived and difficult to sustain. They were most effective when they focused on specific short-run goals, as in the case of the planning for the March on Washington. More general attempts at cooperation ultimately proved evanescent, but at least briefly, they accomplished certain goals. The Council for United Civil Rights Leadership (CUCRL) is a case in point.

CUCRL emerged out of meetings initiated early in 1962 by the white philanthropist Stephen Currier. Seeking guidance for the Taconic Foundation's grant-making in race relations, Currier brought together the leaders of the NAACP, the National Urban League, SNCC, CORE, SCLC, the National Council of Negro Women, and the NAACP Legal Defense and Educational Fund to discuss the racial situation and advise the Foundation on the most effective way to use its resources. The meetings quickly began to serve a broader purpose. By coming together on a regular basis, the leaders became better acquainted with the purposes and activities of the other organizations. The meetings afforded them a chance for reflection and thoughtful analysis, an opportunity to step back from the day-to-day preoccupations of each one's own organization to look at the broad civil rights picture and to examine aspects of the race problem in greater depth and from new perspectives.[3]

The assassination of Medgar Evers in Jackson, Mississippi, in June, 1963, provided the catalyst that transformed the meetings of the leaders into a formal organization. After consulting with a number of the leaders, Currier invited a large group of corporate and foundation executives to breakfast at the Carlyle Hotel in New York City. He asked each civil rights leader to make a statement about his or her organization and its efforts. While the "basic purpose," in the words of the executive director of the Taconic Foundation, was "to get the ears" of the white establishment so that they could "really understand" what was going on, the point was also to raise money for the civil rights movement. The breakfast meeting resulted in pledges of more than $500,000.[4]

With money coming in, there needed to be some sort of a structure to handle disbursements and serve a coordinating function. Building on the foundation laid by their periodic meetings with Currier, the leaders decided to form a new organization. They called it the Council for United Civil Rights Leadership.[5]

CUCRL served two principal functions: raising money for its

constituent organizations and providing a forum for the leaders to share ideas and coordinate strategy. Roy Wilkins, the executive director of the NAACP, called it "a clearing-house to consult, advise and release information about civil rights activities." But there was also a more pointed purpose: to exert a stabilizing (skeptics called it moderating) influence on the movement. As Whitney M. Young, Jr., the executive director of the National Urban League, put it, the idea was "to keep direction of the movement in responsible hands, so it doesn't get 'taken over by some of those fellows waiting in the wings.'"[6]

The promise of "bringing strong, democratic, disciplined and nonviolent leadership" to the civil rights movement proved to be an effective fund-raising device. With $800,000 pledged by mid-July, CUCRL announced a goal of raising $1.5 million by the end of the summer. As the money came in, each organization got its share according to a formula agreed upon by the Council. The emergency funds, which represented a significant addition to the organizations' regular budgets, helped them, a CUCRL spokesman said, to "meet unexpected costs resulting from 'the tremendous increase in civil rights activity across the country'" after those budgets were prepared.[7]

The Council met on a regular basis, at the Carlyle Hotel or at the offices of the Taconic Foundation, the National Urban League, or the Legal Defense Fund. The agendas for the meetings were not in themselves compelling; what was important was that the leaders got together. Fund-raising was a perennial concern, but there was also regular discussion of timely topics—for example, the 1964 Civil Rights Act, other Great Society legislation of special interest to blacks, the Mississippi Summer Project, the Mississippi Challenge. From time to time, the Council spoke as a body to try to influence public policy.[8]

More significant were the opportunities the meetings afforded for sharing information, thinking collectively about the movement, and diminishing tensions among the civil rights organizations. James Farmer, the executive director of CORE, called

CUCRL "a talk group." The leaders would discuss what their organizations had been doing, outline plans for the near future, and suggest ways that other organizations might offer help and cooperation. Dorothy Height, who headed the National Council of Negro Women, reflected on the importance to the leaders of regular opportunities for "thinking and sharing and delving and analyzing and studying." "Our lives were such, we were so busy, either keeping the wolf from the door or going out and dealing with issues and problems," that "we didn't have the time to sit and say, 'What does this mean? And why is it important?' "[9]

Just as periodic discussions gave the leaders a chance to think systematically about the direction of the movement, so they also provided some hope for reducing rivalries and tensions among the organizations. Finding some way to "hold . . . together" a group of leaders who were divided by "a lot of natural, very deep rivalry" had been part of Currier's purpose in creating CUCRL. Discussion of "inter-organizational conflicts," "tensions," and "differences" was a regular agenda item when the Council met. Eliminating competition among the organizations would not have been realistic, but the meetings provided a way to keep tempers and jealousies under better control.[10] John Lewis, chairman of SNCC, credited CUCRL with heading off "major disagreements [and] misunderstandings" among the organizations; it "kept us together," he said, and gave the movement "that sense of unity and focus that it needed during that time."[11]

The civil rights movement had a momentum of its own, which the leaders were not able to control. While it was possible to share plans and describe expectations, what actually happened in the streets could not be planned precisely or promised fully in advance. CUCRL gave the leaders a chance to discuss what had happened and explain why and how it had happened. "It meant," Andrew Young, then of SCLC, reflected, "that there was a place where people could talk through events which they were supposed to be in control of but actually weren't." By providing a "forum where they really understood what was going on, where they got to talk it out," Young said, CUCRL made a contribution to the effectiveness of the movement.[12]

As previously stated, one of the characteristics of formal, organized attempts at cooperation among the leadership was that they ultimately proved evanescent. After a time, it became difficult to hold CUCRL together. Despite repeated reaffirmations of the value of regular contact among the leaders, scheduled meetings became less frequent and attendance dwindled. After the fundraising drive of 1963, there were only modest sums to distribute; by mid-decade, the money had virtually run out. Growing tensions within the movement—over black power, over the desirability of commingling the cause of civil rights with the issue of the United States' role in Vietnam—made unity harder and harder to realize. In January, 1967, steps were taken to liquidate the organization.[13]

CUCRL provides an example of a planned attempt at formal cooperation among civil rights organizations and leaders. Cooperation also emerged without planning or organization, as different organizations and leaders contributed in their own ways to the accomplishment of a single, overriding goal.

In developing models to describe the various roles of protest leaders, social scientists typically elaborate functions that are discharged by different leaders at different stages in the development of social movements. Max Weber identified the "charismatic" leader, whom he contrasted with the "bureaucrat." Harold Lasswell distinguished between the "administrator" and the "agitator." John P. Roche and Stephen Sachs used the terms "bureaucrat" and "enthusiast" to make a similar distinction. Joseph R. Gusfield, taking issue with the prevailing assumption that "statesmanlike, bureaucratic administrators" inevitably replace "enthusiastic, agitational leadership" as social movements "become formally organized into stable structures," posited instead a cyclical alternation between what he called "mobilizing and articulating leadership."[14]

Gusfield's categories serve to establish the basic point about

the different kinds of functions that leaders of social movements
need to discharge. On the one hand, the leader functions as a
mobilizer of commitments to the movement, its "soul and conscience," rallying and inspiring adherents through his single-
minded dedication to the movement, his intransigence toward
groups with different views and interests, and his unwillingness
"to temporize with evil, to compromise principle, or to blunt
sharp controversy." On the other hand, the leader functions as
the articulator of the movement to the larger society, explaining
its purposes to an uncommitted or hostile public, acting as "an
ambassador . . . between the movement and the society," and
using negotiation, bargaining, and compromise to forward the
movement's goals. [15]

In the civil rights movement the functions of bureaucrat and
enthusiast, administrator and agitator, articulator and mobilizer
needed to be discharged simultaneously. Each organization and
leader had different approaches, abilities, resources, and contacts
to bring to bear on the struggle; the complexity of the goals of the
movement demanded that they all be enlisted in order to achieve
the desired progress. As Martin Luther King, Jr., put it, "Direct
action is not a substitute for work in the courts and the halls of
government. Bringing about passage of a new and broad law by a
city council, state legislature or the Congress, or pleading cases
before the courts of the land, does not eliminate the necessity for
bringing about the mass dramatization of injustice in front of a
city hall. Indeed, direct action and legal action complement one
another; when skillfully employed, each becomes more effective." Or, in the words of Whitney Young, "The day has passed
when we could entrust our complete destiny to a single Mes-
sianic leader or rely on any monolithic approach. We must think
today not in terms of individual leaders or of *the* approach—but of
levels of leadership involving many people, with a variety of
approaches and tactics. The issue must now become not *which*
approach, but how we intelligently deploy our forces and establish roles and division of labor." [16]

Young's analysis of the movement's simultaneous dependence on the energies of "older, established" community leaders ("educators, businessmen and professionals"), "confronters" and "protesters," and "strategist[s]" and "planner[s]" hit right on the mark.[17] None could have functioned effectively without the others. SNCC, CORE, and SCLC supplied the charismatic leadership of the movement, rallied and inspired adherents, and organized them for direct-action protests. The NAACP and the National Urban League supplied bureaucratic stability and professional and technical expertise; their leaders functioned as the ambassadors, negotiators, and bargainers who translated the pressure of direct-action protest into concessions from the white power structure. The dichotomy is not precise; the NAACP also played a mobilizing role in communities in the South, and King, the consummate mobilizer, also functioned in critically important ways to articulate the purposes of the movement to white America.

Each organization brought the movement its own distinctive strengths and style. SNCC, the most radical of the direct-action groups, focused on the mobilization and empowerment of local blacks to force change in the status quo; initially committed to direct action and voter registration to break the hold of southern racism, it later rejected nonviolence, interracialism, even capitalism, and called for a radical restructuring of society, with racial separatism and the creation of alternative institutions controlled by the poor and powerless. CORE, pacifist in its origins, working in the North as well as the South, started out as a small, interracial band of disciplined activists determined to apply Gandhian techniques of nonviolent direct action to the problem of American race relations; initially committed to staging dramatic demonstrations to make plain the gross injustice of discrimination and provoke changes in the attitudes and behavior of whites, it later lost faith in the vision of integration and, reformist rather than revolutionary, urged the development of black capitalism and of black control over institutions and services in the ghetto. SCLC, led by ministers, powered by Martin Luther King's vision of a "beloved community," and unwaveringly devoted to integration, initially employed a strategy of nonviolent persuasion to dramatize the evils of discrimination and change the hearts and minds of white oppressors; later, it shifted to a strategy of aggressive nonviolent coercion, designed to provoke retaliatory violence, capture the attention of the media, activate national support for the movement, and thus bring pressure for federal intervention, including the passage of civil rights legislation. By contrast, the NAACP, with its lawyers, lobbyists, and publicists, specialized in legal and legislative action to secure black rights; of all the organizations, it had the best connections in Washington. The National Urban League, a professional social work agency, devoted its efforts to improving the economic and social condition of blacks in the cities. Negotiating with the corporate establishment was its particular strength; of all the organizations, it had the best connections with the major foundations.[18]

Sometimes, as with CUCRL, the marshaling of different leaders and organizations under a common banner was cooperative and intentional; sometimes there was no deliberate coordination or planning, and cooperation entailed nothing more than different leaders and organizations chipping away at the problem on the basis of their own particular strengths and resources. In either case, the point still holds: without the simultaneous enlistment of all of these organizations and leaders, civil rights progress would have been much more difficult to come by.

Several examples illustrate the case. The interplay of direct action and legal action is a persistent theme in the history of the movement. In Montgomery, it took a year-long bus boycott, organized by the Montgomery Improvement Association, as well as a suit carried to the United States Federal District Court and later the United States Supreme Court by lawyers from the NAACP Legal Defense Fund, to desegregate the city's buses in 1956. The sit-ins which spread across the South beginning in 1960 brought the arrests of hundreds of demonstrators; while the sit-ins themselves often brought about the desegregation of lunch counters and other public facilities, it took court cases, often argued by Legal Defense Fund lawyers, to overturn the convictions of the protestors. In Birmingham in 1963, as Martin Luther King developed and executed a successful strategy for direct-action protest, he turned repeatedly to the Legal Defense Fund for money and legal advice; when he, Ralph David Abernathy, Wyatt Tee Walker, and Fred Shuttlesworth went on trial for violating a state-court injunction prohibiting them and other movement leaders from conducting demonstrations, they retained attorneys from the Fund.[19]

At so many points, the success of the movement depended directly on the mobilization of the energies and resources of a range of organizations and leaders. In 1961, for instance, when the original group of Freedom Riders assembled by CORE were so badly beaten in Alabama that they were unable to go any further, SNCC sent in new recruits to help continue the Ride. Subsequently, as mob violence against the Freedom Riders became so severe that the Kennedy administration was forced to send federal marshals to Alabama to help protect them, CORE, SCLC, SNCC, and the Nashville Christian Leadership Council set up a Freedom Ride Coordinating Committee, rejected Attorney General Robert F. Kennedy's call for a temporary suspension of the Rides, and sent the Riders on to Mississippi. When they arrived in Jackson, over 300 were arrested and incarcerated in the city and county jails and the state penitentiary. In an effort to bankrupt CORE, the state of Mississippi manipulated trial dates and tripled the bond on each Rider. The NAACP Legal Defense Fund, with $300,000 in bail-bond money in the bank, came to the rescue with a loan. Later, attorneys for CORE and the Legal Defense Fund appealed the convictions to the United States Supreme Court, which found in favor of the Freedom Riders.[20]

In the case of the 1964 Civil Rights Act, SCLC's demonstrations in Birmingham in April and May, 1963, and the retaliatory violence they precipitated, helped to move President Kennedy to submit comprehensive proposals for civil rights legislation to Congress in June. But while direct action may have changed the public mood and softened the President's previous reluctance to take significant action on civil rights, it was not sufficient to lead Congress to enact the legislation. The introduction of the bill by no means spelled the end of intervention by civil rights leaders and organizations. In the long months that the bill languished in Congress, Clarence Mitchell, the NAACP's chief Washington lobbyist, played a continuing role in influencing the framing of its provisions and the prospects for its passage; finally, in the spring of 1964, Whitney Young and Roy Wilkins weighed in in the successful effort to persuade Senate Minority Leader Everett M. Dirksen to support the bill and bring with him enough Republican votes to break the southern filibuster that was holding up its approval.[21]

The problem of employment discrimination similarly illustrates the way in which different civil rights organizations, complementing each other, brought to bear different resources to pursue a common goal. Before the passage of the 1964 Civil Rights Act, whose Title VII mandated equal employment opportunity, direct action demonstrations—sit-ins, picketing, and boycotts, usually organized by CORE, SNCC, and SCLC—were the major resource the civil rights movement used to attack discrimination in employment. After Title VII the focus changed; individuals who were discriminated against had the right to file complaints with the Equal Employment Opportunity Commission and, in the absence of a satisfactory resolution, to press their claims in federal courts. Now what the movement needed were lawyers to assist in filing complaints and to argue employment discrimination cases in court, a resource supplied by the NAACP. At the same time, employers feeling pressure to comply with Title VII needed help in finding qualified blacks, establishing training programs, and easing the transition to an integrated workplace. Here the National Urban League had the contacts, experience, and trained personnel to provide the necessary assistance.[22]

From time to time the virtues of diversity also proved themselves not in cooperation, whether conscious or de facto, but in the ability to make creative use of competition and disunity, as leaders and organizations played deliberately on the differences within the movement as a tactic to move whites who would otherwise have been less receptive to demands for change. The movement depended on what James Q. Wilson called "a division of labor between protest leaders and bargainers." Asked about the relationship between demonstration and negotiation, James Farmer answered, "They are not contradictory at all—not mutually exclusive. We find that demonstrations are frequently the catalyst—spur the dialogue. Sometimes demonstrations start the dialogue." To put it simply, agitation on the part of militants served to legitimate the demands and modes of protest of more moderate leaders and to enable those moderates to gain the attention of the white establishment and win concessions from the power structure in ways that would not have been possible without that agitation.[23]

Jack L. Walker's study of the student movement in Atlanta in 1960–61 provides an apt illustration of this phenomenon. Responding to the sit-ins that began in Greensboro in February, 1960, Atlanta University students launched demonstrations against segregated lunch counters and businesses that practiced discrimination in hiring. After almost a year of sit-ins, marches, picketing, and boycotts, with repeated but unsuccessful negotiations between students and merchants, the arrest of student demonstrators in February, 1961, and the threat that a planned protest march and rally might result in a riot led student leaders to turn to "one of the oldest, most respected Negro leaders" in Atlanta and ask him "to try to get negotiations started again." Drawing on his friendships with influential whites, he did so, and the resulting negotiations led eventually to a settlement of the controversy.[24]

The division in the black community between the students and their adult supporters, who believed in the efficacy of direct-

action protests, and more conservative black leaders, who agreed
with the students' goals but disagreed with them over the appro-
priateness of demonstrations and boycotts as methods to achieve
them, proved salutary in accomplishing desegregation. "The students and adult protest leaders," Walker writes,

> by organizing demonstrations and economic boycotts, created
> a crisis which had to be resolved. . . . But the leaders of the
> protests did not have the power to resolve the crisis . . .
> because they had no basis for contact with the dominant white
> leaders. . . .
>
> The more conservatively inclined leaders, utilizing their repu-
> tations and the connections they had built up with the white
> community through the years, had the function of resolving the
> crisis situation created by the protest leaders. In this case even
> the antagonism between the two groups was functional because
> it made the conservatives seem more reliable and responsible
> in the eyes of the whites.[25]

The ability to exploit the disunity of the civil rights movement
to accomplish his own ends was part of the stock-in-trade of the
National Urban League's Whitney M. Young. As a social worker
trained to analyze social processes and to understand and relate
to difference, Young was especially well equipped to grasp the
value to the civil rights movement of tensions between moderates
and militants. Dorothy Height spoke about his ability to recognize the interdependence of different approaches, the value of
different roles: "He used to have a way of saying, 'Well, you see,
the more they [the militants] pound on the table, then the
readier other people are to sit at the table and talk to me.' "[26]

Far from crippling the movement, the creative tension between moderates and militants facilitated the accomplishment of
its goals. Without the pressure from direct actionists in the
streets, leaders of the white establishment would have been
much less ready to negotiate with moderate civil rights leaders.
Later, without the rhetoric of black separatism and the resort to
violence, the urgency of addressing fundamental issues of civil
rights and economic opportunity for blacks would have been

much less compelling. Young understood that, and he deliberately used the threat of the militants as a tactic in his dealings with corporate leaders.

John H. Johnson, president of Johnson Publishing Company, remembered with considerable amusement Young's description of his approach. Young told Johnson that he was usually able to gain a hearing from most of the corporate executives he wanted to see. When he had trouble, he would sometimes call Malcolm X and ask *him* to call the executive in question. Suddenly access was no longer a problem; the man always called Young back. "'Whitney, what do you think Malcolm wants with me?'" he might ask. Young would reply, in effect, "'I imagine it would be nice if you were doing something [constructive for blacks] in our community so that you would have an answer to whatever Malcolm has to say.'"27

James Farmer described another variant of Young's technique. Young used "the iron fist of the militants" as "a threatened right cross when his negotiations' left jab failed to produce the desired results," Farmer explained. "'If you don't do what I'm asking you to do,' [Young] would say to corporation heads, 'Jim Farmer and CORE will be coming after you.' The threat usually worked."28

In public, it was unseemly to name names, but with the upsurge of separatism and racial violence, it was easy to communicate a similar point. As Young put it in an address to the Conference Board in 1965, "You must either give support to responsible Negro leadership or else irresponsible leadership will take over." That meant negotiate with the National Urban League, or deal with angry young militants; do something constructive about the race problem, or face the spectre of riots in the streets. With options of that sort, the best choice was clear. In the words of James R. Shepley, the former president of Time, Inc., "I don't think there's any doubt that the average establishmentarian American white would have certainly considered Whitney Young's alternative the best of all possible alternatives that confronted him." As cries of black power grew louder and unrest festered in urban ghettos, businessmen who felt that they had to respond in some way to the race problem looked increasingly to Young and the Urban League for guidance and solutions.[29]

After 1965, opportunities for significant cooperation in the civil rights movement became increasingly rare. Before that, no matter how much leaders and organizations may have differed over strategy and tactics, they shared a commitment to common, realizable objectives: desegregation of public facilities, equal access to education and employment opportunity, full and free exercise of the right to vote. Moroever, they could identify the specific actions necessary to realize those objectives—persuasion of public officials and private individuals, passage of new legislation, prosecution of suits in state and federal courts—and they knew how to rally adherents and mobilize resources to accomplish their ends.

After 1965, disagreement over fundamental objectives as well as strategy and tactics split the movement asunder. The controversy over black power, the issue of racial violence, and the argument over linking the movement to opposition to American involvement in Vietnam created irreparable divisions within the movement. What was at issue was not which organization or leader would claim the credit or win the limelight, nor the best strategy for realizing shared goals. Leaders and organizations no longer agreed even on such basic objectives as integration; and while they may still have shared some general, overriding concerns, the very nature of those concerns—for instance, what to do about black unemployment and underemployment, or how to improve the living conditions of blacks in urban ghettos—meant that there was no longer a consensus on what needed to be done, nor, for that matter, an understanding of the probable efficacy of specific strategies or actions. At the same time that the goals of black protest became more diffuse, the targets of protest activity became less clearly identifiable. With the desegregation of lunch counters or the passage of civil rights legislation, it was easy to figure out which individuals and groups had the power to effect change, and to exert pressure accordingly. Objectives such as the improvement of housing or economic conditions in the ghetto were simply less amenable to that kind of analysis and action.[30]

In such circumstances formal cooperation was unthinkable; without clearly defined, realizable objectives, even the unplanned, informal cooperation by which different organizations and leaders brought to bear their own resources and strengths became much less likely to occur. Only the ability to make creative use of competition persisted into the late 1960s, as the threat of black power and racial violence continued to give more moderate leaders the means to make some headway in their dealings with the white establishment.

Commentary / David J. Garrow

Too often those who write about the civil rights movement employ too narrow and exclusive a concept of "leadership." Implicitly if not explicitly, they presume that leaders are simply those individuals who are organizational chieftains or spokespersons. They thus restrict our definition of leadership to administrators and articulators, without looking as carefully and as thoughtfully as they should for a more meaningful understanding of "leadership."

This overly narrow conception of leadership runs directly parallel to a similar tendency to devote a disproportionate amount of scholarly attention to the national civil rights organizations of the 1950s and 1960s—the National Association for the Advancement of Colored People (NAACP), the Southern Christian Leadership Conference (SCLC), the Student Nonviolent Coordinating Committee (SNCC), the National Urban League (NUL) and the Congress of Racial Equality (CORE). While concentrating studies on those organizations and the individuals who headed them—Roy Wilkins, Martin Luther King, Jr., John Lewis and Stokely Carmichael, Whitney Young, and James Farmer—simultaneously far too little scholarly attention has been devoted to local level civil rights activities and to the grass roots organizers who actually mobilized people to participate actively in the movement.

In the 1950s, the major strategic difference of opinion that existed among black civil rights activists was a division between those who believed that courtroom litigation and judicial decisions were the principal means for advancing black freedom and those who contended that ordinary, grass roots people could take a direct and meaningful hand in pursuing their own freedom. While NAACP Executive Secretary Roy Wilkins and NAACP Legal Defense and Educational Fund director Thurgood Marshall argued that the lawyerly expansion of the principles articulated by the Supreme Court in *Brown* v. *Board of Education of Topeka* was the surest route to further black gains, Brotherhood of Sleeping Car Porters president A. Philip Randolph and other colleagues maintained that mass action, and not simply elite-sponsored litigation, could bring about substantial racial change.

Those mass action proponents welcomed the Montgomery, Alabama, bus boycott of 1955–1956 as precisely the sort of opening round in a new, mass-based southern freedom struggle they long had hoped for. Similarly, those activists also welcomed the 1957 formation of the ministerially-oriented SCLC and the largely spontaneous black college student sit-in movement that spread like wildfire across the South during the spring and early summer of 1960. On the other hand, NAACP administrators contended that it was only a federal court ruling, not the mass boycott, that actually desegregrated Montgomery's buses, and they regretted both the formation of SCLC and the appearance of SNCC, which grew out of the 1960 sit-ins. Within just a few years' time, both SCLC and SNCC, employing different tactical choices, made the mass action strategy the dominant approach of the 1960s black freedom struggle.

That deeply-rooted strategic division is central both to the subsequent history of inter-organizational relations within the movement and to the malapportionment of scholarly attention over the past two decades. Like the one-time chieftains of the elite-oriented civil rights organizations, many scholars have presumed that the policies, statements and actions of the national civil rights organizations are the most importance substance of the movement's history. However, a more discerning look at the movement's actual record of achievement in the south, and in the national political arena, reveals, upon careful examination, that the real accomplishments of the black freedom struggle stemmed not so much from the activities of the administrators and articulators as from the efforts of the grass roots organizers who actually built and directed the movement in the South.

To say that most of the work of the movement was not done by the commonly-identified leaders would seem obvious to all. The basic point, however, is considerably broader than that: what the carefully-scrutinized historical record shows is that the actual human catalysts of the movement, the people who really gave direction to the movement's organizing work, the individuals whose records reflect the greatest substantive accomplishments, were not administrators or spokespersons, and were not those whom most scholarship on the movement identifies as the "leaders." Instead, in any list, long or short, of the activists who had the greatest personal impact upon the course of the southern movement, the vast majority of names will be ones that are unfamiliar to most readers. Allow six brief examples to suffice. In Mississippi, no other individuals did more to give both political direction and emotional sustenance to movement activists than Robert Parris Moses, a SNCC field worker who became the guiding force in COFO, the Council of Federated Organizations, and Fannie Lou Hamer, the relatively unlettered but impressively articulate Sunflower County tenant farmer's wife who in 1964 emerged as an influential grass roots spokeswoman for the thousands of economically poor black citizens who actually comprised the movement's base.

In southwest Georgia, another major scene of movement activism, the guiding spirit of much of the effort there, from the time of his initial arrival in Terrell County as the sole paid field secretary of SNCC to the present day, when he serves on the Albany city council, was Charles Sherrod, a little-heralded organizer who deserves much of the credit for sparking and sustaining the entire southwest Georgia movement. Although Sherrod, like Moses, was an "outside agitator" initially sent in by SNCC, in Selma, Alabama, one of the movement's most famous battlegrounds, the key individual figure was a long-time native, Mrs. Amelia P. Boynton, whose impact there was much like Mrs. Hamer's in Mississippi. A crucial figure in organizing the initial indigenous activism, in first bringing SNCC workers to Selma, and in persuading Dr. King and SCLC to make Selma the focal point of their 1965 voting rights protests, Mrs. Boynton had as substantial an impact on civil rights developments in Alabama as anyone, excepting perhaps only Birmingham's Reverend Fred L. Shuttlesworth, another widely-underestimated and underappreciated grass roots leader.

Lastly, inside of SNCC and SCLC, two individuals who had crucial but often-overlooked roles in repeatedly influencing important movement decisions were Diane Nash and James Bevel, both of whom emerged from the Nashville movement of 1959–1961. Nash played a central part in sustaining the 1961 Freedom Rides when white Alabama violence threatened to halt them, and her April, 1962 memo reprimanding movement activists for not always living up in practice to their much-touted slogan of "jail, no bail" had a significant impact on King and dozens of others. Together with Bevel, Nash in September, 1963, originated one of the most important strategic gameplans of the southern struggle. Four months earlier Bevel, a young SCLC staff aide, had been personally responsible for SCLC's crucial tactical decision to send young children into the streets of Birmingham during the height of the protests there, the crucial turning point in convincing white business leaders to grant the movement's demands and an important influence on President John F. Kennedy's decision to send to Congress the bill that eventually became the 1964 Civil Rights Act. Nash and Bevel, in the immediate aftermath of the Birmingham church bombing that killed four young girls, envisioned a comprehensive mass action campaign to close down the regular functioning of Alabama state government and "GROW"— Get Rid Of [Alabama Governor George C.] Wallace. Though rejected by King and other organization heads at that time, the Nash/Bevel blueprint started King and SCLC on an Alabama Project that eighteen months later, following various changes and refinements, culminated in the landmark Selma-to-Montgomery march and congressional passage of the 1965 Voting Rights Act.

It takes nothing away from King, Wilkins, Whitney Young or James Farmer to acknowledge that Moses, Hamer, Sherrod, Boynton, Nash and Bevel equally merit the designation as civil rights "leaders" if that label is to be applied in its most substantively meaningful way. Indeed, it could be argued further, with considerable justification, that catalytic grass root workers like those six deserve the appellation more than do New York-based bureaucrats such as Wilkins and Young. The real emergence of a sustained and widespread movement in the South can be traced, in many particulars, to the August, 1961, SNCC decision to create a cadre of locally-based, full time grass roots organizers, the first time that indigenous activists in many areas of the rural Deep South had such day-to-day organizational assistance available to them. Those full-time workers, usually affiliated with SNCC, CORE or SCLC, constituted the real backbone of the southern movement during the years of its greatest activism and achievements, 1961–1966. Similarly, the somewhat precipitous decline of the southern freedom struggle between 1966 and 1968 can also largely be traced to the burnout and eventual departure from full time organizing of most of that crucial cadre. Although this is not the place to make the argument in its most extended form, it was the interaction between the existing indigenous activists and these full time field secretaries that generated most of the actual "leadership" of the southern struggle. As many SNCC veterans in particular can well articulate, it was the firsthand experience of working with people, day in, day out, that educated both local activists and field secretaries to the item-by-item, conversation-by-conversation reality of what "leadership" really amounted to in the civil rights movement.

The best of the national organization chieftains and spokespersons, namely King, Lewis and Farmer, all privately appreciated how their heavy responsibilities for making speeches, raising funds, and stimulating organizational publicity oftentimes excessively drew them away from the real, hands on work of the movement. King and Farmer in particular were troubled by how their administrative tasks and the "organization maintenance" needs of SCLC and CORE often took priority over any opportunities for sustained personal involvement in the activities that constituted the real purpose of their organizations. Thus at least these men, if not all of the other administrators and articulators of movement organizations, realized full well that leadership of the freedom struggle lay in many, many hands other than those of the "Big Six" organization heads often singled out by the news media.

A second centrally important aspect of the movement's history, and particularly of the interplay amongst those nationally visible organizations, was the extremely debilitating competition that developed between most of those groups during the 1957–1967 decade. In general, that competition can be divided into two distinct types, organizational and personal. Organizational rivalry was certainly the more powerful and important of the two, centering again and again on two intimately-related maintenance needs of all the national groups: media publicity and the fund-raising opportunities that stemmed from such visibility.

In the late 1950s, the primary face-off was between the newly-formed SCLC and the well-entrenched NAACP, eager to guard its southern branches' local predominance despite the legal attacks being mounted against the Association by many southern state governments. Afraid that SCLC, with King's Montgomery success fresh in the minds of millions, might take the lead in the southern struggle, the NAACP's top national bureaucrats instructed their underlings to avoid and oppose SCLC's nascent voter registration efforts. In 1960, when the NAACP worried that the creation of SNCC would badly undercut its own youth council network and shift the movement's initiative to a younger generation with little interest in following the dictates of a national headquarters, SCLC too thought it would be better for the students to operate as an arm of an established organization—namely SCLC—rather than independently. SNCC in turn complained repeatedly that donations intended for the students instead made their way into SCLC's coffers, and when CORE in 1961 initiated the Freedom Ride, the wave of publicity that followed white attacks on the riders led to intense rivalry between CORE, SNCC and SCLC over claiming credit for sustaining the Rides and apportioning the financial costs and benefits stemming from the Rides. Similar disputes over which organization deserved credit, who would pay the bills, and who was reaping the media publicity troubled or followed virtually every other major southern movement effort of the early and mid 1960s.

Unfortunately, organizational competition for publicity and funds was not the only debilitating type of rivalry that troubled the movement. Additionally, and less understandably, there was also, in some instances, intense personal envy and jealousy on the part of some organization heads towards others. Far and away the strongest, most constant and most important example of such petty personal resentment was the intense antipathy that NAACP executive secretary Roy Wilkins developed for SCLC President Martin Luther King, Jr. Already a strong animus as early as 1957–1958, Wilkins' dislike for King and King's public prominence seems to have stemmed principally from a profound unhappiness that someone other than him, the head of the NAACP, would be viewed by almost all Americans as the primary symbol, spokesman and leader of the civil rights struggle and black America.

What most deserves attention is not the often-unpleasant details of these organizational and personal antipathies, but the extremely debilitating effects these rivalries had in and around the movement. These harmful effects can be categorized under three broad headings: the damage that was done among the national organizations themselves, the harm that was done to local allies and activists, and the impairments these tensions caused the movement with actual and potential "external" supporters such as white church groups, labor chieftains and federal government officials. Within the major civil rights groups, a dismaying amount of time, energy and effort was devoted to fanning, parrying or otherwise coping with these internecine conflicts. Although some civil rights staffers, such as Wilkins and Gloster Current of the NAACP, seem—based on their own surviving office files in the NAACP Papers at the Library of Congress—to have positively enjoyed such private verbal attacks on movement colleagues, even for those activists who loathed and avoided such negative jousting, the petty bickering constituted a regular distraction and wasteful diversion.

Often more dismaying and painful was the effect that these interorganizational conflicts had on indigenous local activists who were at first puzzled and then depressed as the reality of national group rivalries became clear to them. In Albany in 1961–1962, in Jackson in 1963, and in many other locales throughout the early and mid-1960s, local black civic activists learned again and again that some of the national civil rights groups, the NAACP in particular, on occasion expended as much energy in competing with other movement organizations as in combatting segregation.

Perhaps most harmfully for the movement, these internal rivalries had a considerable impact—oftentimes an excessive impact—on allied white organizations, which sometimes seem to have cited these internecine problems as grounds—or as an excuse—for moderating the amount of active support they would offer for movement initiatives. Even more notably, the movement's splits also became a prime topic of discussion and analysis within the uppermost reaches of the federal government. Justice

Department aides and White House staffers repeatedly pondered how to respond to initiatives from King or Wilkins in such a way as to not offend one or the other; at the height of the Birmingham crisis, as President Kennedy and his top Cabinet officers considered what actions to take, Attorney General Robert Kennedy reminded his brother and the others present that they had to take into account the fact that "Roy Wilkins hates Martin Luther King" (White House Tape #88-4, 5/20/63, JFK Library).

Professor Nancy Weiss is correct to emphasize that the multiplicity of civil rights organizations often worked to the strategic political advantage of the movement; white officials at both the local and federal level often dealt more responsively with some black spokesmen, such as King and Wilkins, simply because they were fearful of otherwise having to cope with more "radical" elements in the movement, particularly SNCC. On one occasion, John Kennedy went so far as to tell a visiting delegation of white Birmingham leaders that they ought to be thankful, rather than upset, at having Martin Luther King and SCLC focusing upon their city; otherwise, Kennedy warned, they would be faced with those "sons of bitches" in SNCC who had "an investment in violence" (White House Tape #112-6, 9/23/63, JFK Library).

Professor Weiss also is correct to focus considerable attention on "CUCRL," the Council for United Civil Rights Leadership, an important movement forum whose role has often been misconstrued when not ignored altogether. Nonetheless, it is essential to appreciate the admixture of motives that lay behind the mid-1963 creation of CUCRL: first, a firm desire on the part of wealthy white movement supporters such as Taconic Foundation President Stephen R. Currier to stabilize if not eliminate the increasingly visible and hostile competition between civil rights groups for contributors' dollars; second, a wish to moderate the southern movement's increasingly aggressive and demanding tone by giving NAACP chief Wilkins and National Urban League head Whitney Young, a good friend of Currier's, a regular and intimate forum for propounding their views to the more direct action-oriented leaders of SNCC, CORE and SCLC; and, third, an intent to exert some amount of control over SNCC's angriest inclinations by centralizing at least a part of movement fund-raising and using the resulting allocation process as a carrot-and-stick inducement for SNCC to follow a "responsible" course.

While Professor Weiss may be overestimating the positive value that the CUCRL discussion meetings had for at least a good number of civil rights organization heads, several of whom often sent deputies rather than attend in person, it is more important to recognize and appreciate CUCRL for what it was, a modestly-successful and relatively short-lived response to the centrifugal, competitive tensions within the civil rights movement that even as early as 1963 threatened to rend the black freedom struggle into openly divided camps. Although in large part that public break was postponed until mid-1966, scholars would err if they excessively minimized the deleterious effects that the move-ment's internal divisions were having even well before that time. Just as they must avoid an overly-narrow conception of leadership and an excessive focus of their research attentions on the na-tionally-oriented civil rights organizations alone, so must they also, when they do look at those groups and their top executives, do so with an analytically critical eye that allows them to weigh accurately, rather than overstate, the contributions that those organizations made to the black freedom struggle during the 1950s and 1960s.

The Politics of the Mississippi Movement, 1954–1964

JOHN DITTMER

In May of 1963 two Mississippi leaders appeared on local television to discuss race relations in the state's capital city. Jackson was then in the midst of crisis. A black boycott of downtown merchants over the issues of jobs and segregation had led to mass rallies, demonstrations, and picketing. Refusing to negotiate, city officials were trying to break the movement by filling the jails with civil rights activists. For Mayor Allan Thompson, there was simply nothing to negotiate about. In his television appeal to "our Nigra citizens," the mayor reminded blacks of their good fortune in being Jacksonians:

> You live in a city, a beautiful city, where you can send your children to modern schools, you live in homes that are clean and neat with all utilities. And [as] I have said, there are no slums [in Jackson] as there are in most other large cities.

Warming to his subject, the mayor could hardly contain his enthusiasm:

> You have 24-hour protection by the police department. Just think of being able to call the police any time of the night and say, "Come quick! Someone is trying to get into my house, I need some help". . . . You live in a city where you can work, where you can make a comfortable living. You are treated, no matter what anybody tells you, with dignity, courtesy, and respect. Ah, what a wonderful thing it is to live in this city![1]

For Medgar Evers, the reality was somewhat different. Given equal time to reply to Mayor Thompson, the NAACP state field secretary observed that when a black Jacksonian looks about his home community,

> He sees a city where Negro citizens are refused admittance to the city auditorium and the coliseum; his wife and children refused service in a downtown store where they trade; students refused the use of the main library, parks, and other tax-supported recreational facilities. . . . He sees a city of over 150,000, of which 40 percent is Negro, in which there is not a single Negro policeman or policewoman, school crossing guard, or fireman. . . . The mayor spoke of the 24-hour police protection we have. Well, there are questions in the minds of many Negroes whether we have 24 hours of protection, or 24 hours of harassment.

Evers went on to explain to the TV audience just "what the Negro wants":

> He wants to get rid of racial segregation in Mississippi life. . . . The Negro wants to register and vote without special handicaps imposed on him alone. . . . The Negro Mississippian wants more jobs above the menial level in stores where he spends his money. He wants the public schools and colleges desegregated so that his children can receive the best education that Mississippi has to offer.

The NAACP leader concluded his talk with an "appeal to the consciences of many silent, responsible citizens of the white community who know that a victory for democracy in Jackson will be a victory for democracy everywhere."[2]

Medgar Evers's address reflected the thinking of the men and women who, a decade earlier, had launched the modern freedom struggle in Mississippi. Theirs was not a revolutionary movement. They were asking that white people live up to the ideals they openly professed, what Gunnar Myrdal had called "the American creed of progress, liberty, equality, and humanitarianism" embodied in the Declaration of Independence and the United States Constitution.[3] But white southerners had been unmoved by appeals to conscience and patriotism. Mayor Thompson spoke for the vast white majority in his determination to preserve the status quo in his city. His remarks were ludicrous, but tragic in their implications. If Byron de La Beckwith pulled the trigger that ended Medgar Evers's life less than a month later, a whole society stood indicted for the crime.

Nineteen sixty-three was a year of turmoil for the Mississippi movement. Efforts to organize black communities had met with fierce white opposition, and many local people had become disillusioned, convinced that the American Dream was also reserved "for whites only." Veteran black activists were now openly questioning, along with James Baldwin, whether they really wanted to integrate "a burning house." Viewed in a broader perspective, then, the civil rights movement had been a referendum on the principles of American liberalism, whether this country could at last resolve Myrdal's "dilemma" over the theory and practice of democracy. For over a century black Mississippians had been struggling to realize that democratic promise, only to find white America not yet committed to acting upon its principles by enforcing its laws in the Closed Society.

In a sense the modern civil rights movement in Mississippi began in a courtroom in Washington, D.C. The *Brown* decision of May 1954 provided both a rallying cry and a focus for black men and women working for social change, and the subsequent white defiance of the law initiated a period of racial confrontation unmatched since the latter days of Reconstruction. But the black struggle for freedom in Mississippi did not spring up overnight. The leadership of the early movement was forged on the battlefields of World War II and grounded in indigenous institutions in the black community such as the church, the handful of private black colleges, and the family. And while the folklore of the movement has fastened upon the heroic example of outstanding individuals—Fannie Lou Hamer, Medgar Evers, Bob Moses— from the outset the Mississippi movement operated within the framework of established organizations for racial advancement, both local and national.

For over three decades prior to the 1950s, black civil rights activity in Mississippi had been synonymous with the National Association for the Advancement of Colored People. Organized in Vicksburg in 1918, by the early fifties the NAACP claimed 1600 members in twenty-one chapters.[4] Throughout its formative period the NAACP had kept a low profile, for fear of white reprisal limited membership and restricted activities to quiet efforts to register black voters. But World War II had brought social and economic changes to the Magnolia State, along with a cadre of veterans who returned home fighting. Small businessmen, farm owners, and the handful of black professionals, men like Amzie Moore, Aaron Henry, and Medgar Evers quickly rose to positions of community leadership. The civil rights vanguard in the decade after World War II, then, was largely male, middle class, and at least marginally free from white economic control. They comprised the backbone of the NAACP chapters operating throughout the state.

The first major test for the new civil rights forces came in the wake of the Supreme Court decision outlawing segregation in the nation's public schools. Unable to coopt black leaders, white spokesmen breathed defiance. At the heart of the white resistance was the Citizens' Council, an organization of middle class men dedicated to maintaining white supremacy, whatever the cost. While Council leaders stressed the "legality" of their methods, members of this "uptown Ku Klux Klan" often took the law into their own hands, acting as judge and jury in punishing blacks daring to challenge the caste system.[5]

The strategy for desegregating public schools in Mississippi originated with the NAACP. In keeping with its traditional legalistic approach, the NAACP took no direct action until the Supreme Court issued its implementation decree.[6] When that decision came down in May of 1955 blacks filed school desegregation petitions in Jackson, Vicksburg, Yazoo City, Natchez, and Clarksdale, cities with active NAACP chapters. In each community the local Citizens' Council crushed the petition drive. In Yazoo City the Council took out full-page advertisements in the newspaper, listing the names and addresses of the fifty-three parents petitioning for an end to school segregation. Almost immediately those petitioners working for white people lost their jobs, while independent entrepreneurs were forced out of business. Within a short time all but two of the signers had removed their names from the list, and both of the remaining signatories soon left the city. Membership in the Yazoo City NAACP dropped off sharply, while the local Citizens' Council grew from a base of sixteen founders to an organization of over 1500 card-carrying members. Similar tactics produced the same results in the other cities targeted for desegregation.[7]

The NAACP was ill-equipped to combat the Citizens' Council's counter-offensive. It had underestimated the ferocity of white resistance, and overestimated the federal government's commitment to law enforcement. The Eisenhower administration stood by while Mississippi whites made a mockery of the *Brown* decision, and repeated pleas by local and national NAACP officials met a wall of federal indifference.[8] NAACP state field secretary Medgar Evers worked tirelessly to mobilize blacks in communities across Mississippi, but events were moving too quickly, and all Evers and local leaders could do was to enlist courageous citizens to assume the risks inherent in directly challenging white supremacy. Given the powerful segregationist opposition, the inaction of the federal government, and the lack of a deep base of support in the black community, the petitioners were sitting ducks, to be picked off one by one by the sharpshooters of the Citizens' Council.

With the school desegregation movement stopped in its tracks, blacks shifted their focus to winning the right to vote. Mississippi's million blacks comprised 45 percent of the state population, the highest percentage in the nation. Yet only about 22,000 (just four percent of the voting-age group) were registered in

1954.[9] Since the late nineteenth century whites had used the poll tax, discriminatory registration requirements, intimidation and violence to keep blacks from voting. But encouraged by the broader implications of *Brown*, blacks in 1955 mounted voter registration programs across the state. Local NAACP chapters took the lead, assisted in some areas by the Regional Council of Negro Leadership, founded in 1950 by Dr. T. R. M. Howard, a Mound Bayou physician and businessman.

Again whites responded aggressively. Some registrars simply turned away black applicants; others refused to accept their poll taxes. Economic retaliation was common, as when a black principal in Tallahatchie County lost his job after attempting to register. And during the 1955 gubernatorial primary the chairman of the Democratic State Committee sent word to all county commissioners that black voters should be challenged on the grounds they were not qualified members of the Mississippi Democratic Party.[10] If these coercive measures failed, whites could impose and carry out the ultimate penalty. In Belzoni, NAACP branch president Reverend George W. Lee was gunned down by a carload of whites. His friend and fellow activist, Gus Courts, survived an assassination attempt, but had to flee the state.[11]

The most blatant political execution in that bloody year of 1955 took place in broad daylight on a busy Saturday afternoon on the courthouse lawn in Brookhaven. The victim was Lamar Smith, 60, a farmer who "had been very active in the political circles of Lincoln County." Although the sheriff saw a white man leaving the scene with "blood all over him," and scores of residents were on the square at the time, no one would admit to having witnessed the shooting. Governor Hugh White refused to intervene, even when requested to do so by local authorities, claiming that "politics is causing the entire mess." There were no convictions in any of the cases.[12] These politically-inspired crimes, along with the lynching of young Emmett Till for allegedly whistling at a white woman, led one white Mississippian to conclude that "There's open season on Negroes now . . . any peckerwood who wants to can go shoot himself one, and we'll free him. Our situation will get worse and worse."[13]

The combination of economic intimidation and physical violence had dealt a severe blow to movement efforts in Mississippi. Local NAACP branches reported membership losses, and fear of white reprisal had forced a number of key activists to move away from the state. Field secretary Medgar Evers worked feverishly to keep the movement alive, criss-crossing the state giving "pep talks" and attempting to allay fears through his own example. But the results were not heartening.[14]

Movement unity was essential during this critical early period, but such efforts were often frustrated by the NAACP hierarchy, which jealously protected its turf in Mississippi and looked upon other civil rights groups with a suspicion bordering on paranoia. The Regional Council of Negro Leadership, whose membership and program overlapped with that of the NAACP, was to be kept at arm's length. NAACP Southeast Regional Secretary Ruby Hurley warned Executive Secretary Roy Wilkins that "extreme care" be exercised in relations with RCNL's T. R. M. Howard, who "is not, nor do I believe he ever will be, a friend of the NAACP." Hurley worried that Medgar Evers "seems to have too much of the Howard influence," and when Evers proposed a merger of the RCNL and the state NAACP, Hurley flatly refused to consider the suggestion, for the Council "was a threat which I have been trying to combat."[15]

Local NAACP activists were far more open to cooperation, for their numbers were small and they welcomed the participation of other groups. Medgar Evers attended the founding convention of the Southern Christian Leadership Conference in 1957 and was elected to its board, but then reluctantly resigned due to pressure from the New York NAACP headquarters.[16] Aaron Henry was even more ecumenical in his approach, serving on the SCLC board and assuming leadership in the RCNL after Dr. Howard was forced from the state. As the unpaid president of the state NAACP, Henry had more independence than Evers, and he exerted it

well into the 1960s. Medgar Evers eventually towed the line,
bowing to the dictates of his superiors. Thus in January of 1958,
when the Mississippi movement was at its lowest ebb, Evers
moved to block SCLC efforts to move into Jackson, reporting to
Ruby Hurley that "we have naturally discouraged . . . any such
movement here. . . . I shall await comments from you. In the
meantime, we are going to hold fast."[17] Mississippi, in short, was
NAACP territory, and emergent civil rights organizations were not
welcome.

As the 1950s drew to a close the NAACP remained the dominant
protest group in Mississippi. But its legalistic approach to the
race problem had proven ineffective in a society which did not
recognize the rule of law. The crushing defeats suffered in the
early school desegregation and voter registration campaigns left
the NAACP without a program. It no longer knew what to do in
Mississippi, so it drew back. Membership drives and inspira-
tional speeches from national leaders replaced community action.
The NAACP was determined to survive in Mississippi, but it was
reluctant to change, and it stubbornly resisted the new tactics of
non-violent direct action. There had been no counterpart to the
Montgomery bus boycott, and the sit-in movement of 1960 had
largely passed Mississippi by. The fanatical white resistance was,
of course, a powerful argument against such protests, but despite
the terror, a new generation of black Mississippians was ready to
move. More impatient than their elders, high school and college
students were eager to push forward with a program of direct
action. Their frustration with the NAACP holding action in Mississippi was shared by a number of older activists, who had by
now become convinced that if the Mississippi movement were to
regain its momentum, reinforcements would be needed from the
outside.[18]

The second wave of the Mississippi movement began with the
Freedom Rides in 1961 and ended at the Democratic National
Convention in Atlantic City in the summer of 1964. In many ways

this new burst of activism was consistent with the initial stirrings of the 1950s. Older, middle-class leaders supplied the base for movement activities in their communities, feeding and housing civil rights workers and offering them a degree of protection. After early misgivings, key black churches opened their doors to the movement, providing both a forum for discussion and, equally as important, the spiritual sanction of the black community's most influential institution. The basic thrust of the movement remained, as it had been for nearly a century, that of voter registration. Operating from an indigenous base in the black community, and building on the earlier struggles of local activists, the movement of the sixties exhibited a degree of continuity with that of the 1950s often overlooked by contemporary observers who "discovered" Mississippi in 1961.

Still, the contrasts between the two decades are striking. The movement of the fifties had been based in the cities, dominated by the NAACP, and centered around the small black middle class. (For example, few black sharecroppers signed school petitions or were encouraged to attempt to register and vote.) Organizers in the 1960s, on the other hand, saw the rural poor as their natural constituency. Young activists abandoned coats and ties for denim overalls in a symbolic effort to identify with the majority of the state's black citizens. And, where in the fifties black men had dominated local leadership, now women were entering the movement in large numbers. They became the backbone of the struggle, comprising a majority at most mass meetings and participating in all phases of activity, from running for Congress to serving time in prison. While the new movement did not succeed in eliminating all distinction by class and gender, it came closer to the ideal of an egalitarian community than has any major American social movement, before or since.

The most visible change in the 1960s was the influx of newcomers ("outside agitators," in the parlance of the Citizens' Council). Black men and women in their teens and twenties, these organizers represented the Congress of Racial Equality (CORE) and, most noticeably, the Student Nonviolent Coordinating Committee (SNCC). Preaching the new doctrine of participatory democracy, they recruited and joined with local people to become the vanguard of the new movement. The presence of these emergent protest groups would cause inter-organizational problems, but until Atlantic City tensions were kept under control, in large part because of the establishment of a civil rights body unique to Mississippi, the Conference of Federated Organizations, or COFO.*

COFO represented an honest and for the most part successful effort to unify all national, state, and local protest groups operating in Mississippi. Historically, COFO has been viewed as little more than a "paper organization," an umbrella agency set up primarily to facilitate the transfer of funds from the Voter Education Project in Atlanta to groups working in the state. COFO directors Dave Dennis and Bob Moses take sharp issue with this characterization, pointing out that although all the national civil rights groups were wary of COFO, black Mississippians "wanted to have the feeling that all of their organizations were working together," and developed strong loyalty to COFO as an entity which belonged to them.[19] All the major black activist organizations were represented in COFO, but SNCC soon emerged as the dominant partner, and its organizers set the tone for the movement of the sixties.[20]

A final point of contrast between the activists of the sixties and their predecessors was ideological. The NAACP leaders of the 1950s generally looked to the liberal wing of the national Democratic Party for support. Having come of age during the New Deal, older black activists believed that change would have to come gradually, under the watchful eye of a strong and active federal government. Few of them were political radicals. Their goal was "simply" to abolish all forms of racial discrimination in

*For the sake of brevity, unless otherwise noted the term "COFO" will describe the activities of the more militant SNCC-CORE faction of the Mississippi movement during the early sixties.

the state, so that blacks might obtain their fair share of the American Dream.

Many younger COFO activists went into the movement committed to this liberal philosophy. Coming out of the church, they were dedicated to the ideals of nonviolence. And while they wanted "more than a hamburger," they were too busy fighting for survival on the back roads of Mississippi to afford time for study and reflection on the inequities inherent in American capitalism. But field experience radicalized movement organizers. Working in the most poverty-stricken sections of America, they came to see that elimination of racial segregation, even getting the vote, would not fundamentally change the lives of the black poor.

At the same time, SNCC and CORE workers were rapidly losing faith in liberal institutions, particularly that of the federal government. Movement archives and interviews with sixties' activists reveal that what angered organizers most was not the behavior of white racists—for this was expected—but rather the failure of the federal government to enforce the United States Constitution in Mississippi. (Perhaps the most vividly recalled image of the federal presence is the scene where a movement worker is being beaten by a white mob while a Justice Department representative stands passively by taking notes.) But in the early sixties movement workers could not afford to turn their backs on the federal government, for only the possibility of federal intervention had restrained white Mississippi from taking even more drastic action against the movement. An increased federal presence, activists believed, would help break down the fear and isolation which kept many blacks from enlisting in the struggle.

Thus the Mississippi movement was forced to operate on two levels. The major task was to continue grass-roots organizing, working quietly and patiently to develop local leadership. At the same time the movement needed to attract publicity for its cause to create public demand that the federal government take action. These two thrusts—low-key, long-term organizing; and dramatic exposure of white lawlessness in areas where the movement was operating—were in a sense contradictory, creating internal tensions which surfaced during the debate over bringing in hundreds of northern volunteers during the summer of 1964.

The major COFO organization and mobilization campaigns of the early sixties: the SNCC projects in McComb and in the Delta; the NAACP boycotts and demonstrations in Clarksdale and Jackson and CORE's voter registration drive in Madison County are in themselves of tremendous importance to the history of the civil rights movement, and each deserves intensive investigation. In looking at this critical period the focus will be on the interaction between the Mississippi movement and the Kennedy administration, a relationship which had an important impact on the evolution of the freedom struggle across the state.

Both John and Robert Kennedy admired the courage of the Mississippi organizers and shared their goal of opening the Closed Society. During its brief tenure the Kennedy administration made its presence felt in the state on several occasions, most notably in the crisis surrounding the desegregation of the University of Mississippi. But the Kennedys wanted to avoid crises and preferred to remain in the background, hoping they might quietly persuade reasonable white Mississippi leaders to obey the law. Leslie Dunbar, then head of the Southern Regional Council, has perceptively observed that in the Kennedy administration there was "a great reluctance . . . to accept the fact that you had to be on somebody's side in the South."[21] As politicians, the Kennedys turned to their kind in times of crisis. When the Freedom Riders were about to journey into Mississippi in the late spring of 1961 Robert Kennedy went to Senator James Eastland for advice, later recalling that "I talked to him probably seven or eight or twelve times each day about what was going to happen when they got to Mississippi and what needed to be done."[22] Using Eastland and former Governor James P. Coleman as intermediaries, the Kennedy administration worked out the compromise that in return for the state's promise to protect the riders from mob violence, the White House would not interfere while local police arrested the Freedom Riders once they stepped off the bus. This despite the fact that the arrests, in Assistant Attorney General Burke Marshall's opinion, "were unconstitutional . . . without any question."[23] The manner in which the Kennedys handled the Freedom Rider crisis set their pattern for the next three years. In situations demanding White House action, they preferred to work behind the scenes with Mississippi officials, avoiding direct involvement with movement activists, a preference which "made Negroes feel like pawns in a white man's political game."[24]

The Kennedys' objective in the Freedom Rides, to prevent violence, became the keystone of their Mississippi policy. They were convinced that strong federal support for civil rights activists in the exercise of their constitutional rights would bring on another civil war in Mississippi, with dire consequences for the South and the nation. Burke Marshall attempted to justify this policy on Constitutional grounds, invoking the doctrine of "federalism," which had as its basic premise that "the responsibility for the preservation of law and order, and the protection of citizens against unlawful conduct on the part of others is the responsibility of the local authorities."[25] Only when a situation deteriorated beyond a point where local officials could control it—as when James Meredith enrolled at Ole Miss—would the federal government respond with outside force. Criticized on legal grounds by scores of attorneys and law school deans, who cited a number of legal precedents for government protection of civil rights workers, the administration nonetheless stood its ground. "We didn't have the power," Burke Marshall later told an interviewer. "And," he added candidly, "we didn't want it."[26]

For a time, though, it had appeared that the Kennedy administration might be willing to protect civil rights activists, particularly those involved in voter registration. When SNCC workers were about to launch the first major voting drive of the sixties in McComb, Marshall sent a memorandum to presidential advisor

Byron White, which concluded that "It must be anticipated that economic and other types of reprisals may occur. If they do, we will have to move immediately to prevent the reprisals through court orders which may have to be enforced by federal marshals."[27] Two months later the beating and arrest of SNCC worker John Hardy brought Justice Department lawyer John Doar quickly to the scene. Doar sought to enjoin the county from bringing Hardy to trial, contending that his prosecution would intimidate potential black registrants. When the Court of Appeals upheld the government's position Robert Kennedy reported to his brother that "this has been a most important decision."[28] Yet as the level of white violence increased in southwest Mississippi the federal government immediately backed away from its activist role. When Amite County organizer Herbert Lee was shot and killed by a member of the state legislature, the Justice Department investigated but took no action. Between 1961 and the fall of 1964 the Justice Department would file twenty-five suits involving discrimination against black registrants. But all had been stalled in the courts, and white repression of voting rights continued unabated.[29] With one partial exception, the Kennedy administration avoided immediate confrontation with local authorities over the issue of protection of blacks attempting to obtain the franchise.

That exception was in Greenwood in 1963, where SNCC was in the middle of its most aggressive voter registration drive. Whites had responded ferociously, severely wounding SNCC worker Jimmy Travis in an assassination attempt, burning the SNCC offices, and arresting blacks attempting to register. On March 31, the Justice Department went into federal court with a petition for a restraining order against local officials, demanding that they release eight movement organizers from prison, refrain from further interference with the registration campaign, and "permit Negroes to exercise their constitutional right to assemble for peaceful protest demonstrations and protect them from whites who might object."[30] This was precisely the type of federal court action Mississippi activists had been hoping for. But less than a week later the Justice Department cut a deal with Greenwood officials, withdrawing the injunction in return for the release of the eight prisoners and a vague promise not to inhibit further registration attempts. Again, fear of white violence was a motivating factor in the decision to compromise. As movement historians Pat Watters and Reece Cleghorn said of the Greenwood agreement, "The threat of lawlessness, then, would rout the federal government in a showdown on the most basic right of American citizenship. This point . . . seemed largely lost on the nation, but not on the white and Negro principals in the showdown."[31]

By the end of the summer of 1963 the Mississippi movement had been stalled on every front. The direct action campaign in Jackson, dealt a severe blow by the death of Medgar Evers, ground to a halt after the Kennedys personally negotiated a behind-the-scenes agreement with Mayor Thompson, who made token concessions in return for an end to the demonstrations.[32] In Clarksdale, where Aaron Henry had built a broad-based local movement and had encouraged participation by all civil rights organizations, whites simply drew the line, refused to negotiate any of the black demands, and kept the jails full of demonstrators. And in Greenwood, where the movement had been strongest, white officials, having backed down the federal government, now felt confident that they could handle anything SNCC could throw at it. It was almost as though it were 1955 all over again. The season was still open on Negroes in Mississippi, and it appeared to most whites that they could crush the movement without fear of outside intervention. But black activists were determined to find a way to gain the freedom to organize their communities. To do so, a change in tactics was necessary.

The new strategy took shape in the summer of 1963 with a COFO decision to hold a state-wide mock election, and culminated in the challenge of the Freedom Democratic Party at the Democratic National Convention in August of 1964. The purpose of the "freedom vote" was both to dramatize black disfranchise-

ment in Misissippi to the rest of the country and to introduce the
movement to new areas of the state. COFO nominated NAACP
state president Aaron Henry for governor and Edwin King, white
chaplain at Tougaloo College, for lieutenant governor. To get out a
large vote, SNCC sent all available staff to Mississippi. They were
assisted in the final weeks of the campaign by white students from
Yale and Stanford recruited by Allard Lowenstein, a white attorney and political activist who first suggested the idea for a
freedom vote. The mock election was a success, with over 80,000
blacks casting ballots for the Henry-King ticket, despite widespread white harassment.[33] Yet the national media had given the
election limited attention (what coverage there was dealt mainly
with the white students), and the pattern of repression in Mississippi continued unabated into 1964. By then COFO had made
tentative plans for a state-wide summer project.

The decision to have a "freedom summer" in Mississippi
deeply divided COFO, both encouraged and alarmed northern
supporters of the movement, and set in motion a series of events
which would eventually divide the movement along race and
class lines. Plans for the summer project called for continued
voter registration efforts, the opening of community centers, the
establishment of "freedom schools," and organization of the new
Freedom Democratic Party for its convention challenge. Most
controversial was the proposal, supported by the COFO leadership, to bring in hundreds of outside volunteers (most of them
white) to help staff the project.

Opposition to the volunteers centered around such veteran
SNCC activists from Mississippi as Willie Peacock and Hollis
Watkins, who believed that the movement should stick to what it
did best: community organizing. They maintained that white
volunteers would inhibit the efforts to build black consciousness
and to develop indigenous, independent leadership.[34] Others
were concerned that the presence of whites in black neighborhoods would attract attention and threaten the security of the
community, or that white college students, confident of their

superior technical skills, would attempt to take over leadership positions.

The major argument for the volunteer presence was tactical: unless America was awakened to what was going down in Mississippi, white Mississippians would destroy the movement of the sixties just as they had the movement of the fifties, through brute force and terror. Bob Moses recalls that he decided to push hard for bringing in the volunteers after learning of the murder of Lewis Allen in southwest Mississippi early in 1964: "There was no real reason to kill Lewis, and they . . . gunned him down on his front lawn. . . . We were just defenseless, there was no way of bringing national attention. . . . And it seemed to me like we were just sitting ducks . . . people were just going to be wiped out."[35] So long as it was black people being brutalized, white Americans would pay little heed. But "they would respond to a thousand young white college students," CORE's Dave Dennis believed. "What we were trying to do was to get a message over to the country, so we spoke their language. And that had more to do with the decision to bring 'em in . . . than anything else."[36] White volunteers would bring visibility and publicity, and might force a reluctant federal government to intervene directly to protect organizers working in the state.

The news of the summer project did not go down well in the national offices of the NAACP. Roy Wilkins and Gloster Current, Director of Branches, had always been uncomfortable with COFO, and the important role their man Aaron Henry was playing in it. At one point Current grumbled to Wilkins that COFO "has captured the imagination and most of the time of our state president, who offers little to his own organization except lip service." Current then added, revealingly: "[Henry] believes that whosoever frees him and his people should be used."[37] During the middle of freedom summer Current had written Charles Evers, who had taken his slain brother's place as state field secretary, advising him that "Every effort should be made to encourage Dr. Henry to wean himself away from [COFO]," con-

cluding ominously that "We shall review our relationship with
that outfit at the end of the summer."[38]

Freedom summer drew a mixed response from white liberals.
The National Council of Churches was enthusiastic about the
project, and financed the two-week training sessions for volunteers in Ohio. The project also drew support from groups of
college professors, lawyers, and physicians, a number of whom
came to Mississippi during the summer to offer their services.
But such influential liberals as Al Lowenstein were disturbed by
COFO's growing radicalism, demonstrated by its failure to exclude
volunteers with leftist backgrounds, and by its decision to invite
the National Lawyers Guild, an avowedly radical organization, to
work with the movement during the summer.

The new administration of Lyndon Johnson adopted a hands-off
policy toward the summer project, refusing to meet either with
COFO leaders or with a delegation of the volunteers' parents.[39]
Both groups were lobbying for federal protection for the project
workers, and Johnson, like his predecessor, opposed the idea. Yet
the administration was well aware of the potential for violence.
Burke Marshall had made a trip to Mississippi during the first
week of June, and was alarmed both at the increase of Klan
activity and by the failure of the FBI to do its job. Marshall
recently observed that prior to freedom summer the Bureau "just
wouldn't put any resources into [Mississippi], and they weren't
any good, and they didn't have any informants."[40] The day after
Marshall returned from his trip, Attorney General Robert Kennedy wrote President Johnson that "I told you in our meeting
yesterday that I considered the situation in Mississippi to be very
dangerous. Nothing in the reports I have received since then
changes my view on that point."[41]

In its broad outline the story of freedom summer is a familiar
one: the orientation sessions in Oxford, Ohio, where the volunteers had to come to grips with their own prejudices; the murders
of Chaney, Schwerner, and Goodman, which cast a pall over the
entire project; the intense activity in the forty-seven freedom

schools and in numerous community centers. Statistics tell part of the story: a thousand arrests; thirty-five shooting incidents; thirty homes and other buildings bombed; thirty-five churches burned; eighty persons beaten; and, in addition to the Neshoba County lynchings, at least three other murders. Freedom summer had brought Mississippi to center stage, both in the nation and throughout the world.[42]

On July 19 Bob Moses sent out an "Emergency Memorandum" urging that "*everyone* who is not working in Freedom Schools or community centers *must* devote all their time to organizing for the [Freedom Democratic Party] convention challenge."[43] The idea for the FDP had come out of the freedom vote campaign, and the state-wide party formally organized in the spring of 1964. Plans were then made to send a delegation to Atlantic City to challenge the seating of the all-white regular Democratic delegation. FDP organizers saw this both as an opportunity to keep the national spotlight on Mississippi and as a dramatic recruiting device to attract more local blacks into the movement. FDP's goal was both to unseat the regulars and to gain official recognition as the legitimate Mississippi delegation.

The Freedom Democratic Party's challenge at Atlantic City served as the culmination of freedom summer and represented a turning point in the civil rights movement. It was the major story at the convention, played out before a television audience of millions of Americans. Although assured of his party's nomination, Lyndon Johnson feared that a floor fight over the Mississippi challenge might lead to a walkout by delegations from Dixie and give momentum to the white backlash vote for Republican Barry Goldwater. Johnson worked tirelessly behind the scenes to thwart the FDP effort. The Freedom Democrats, with their chief counsel, liberal white attorney Joseph Rauh, presented a convincing case, highlighted by the moving testimony of Mrs. Fannie Lou Hamer to the Credentials Committee. (President Johnson was so upset at the live TV coverage of Mrs. Hamer's compelling indictment of Mississippi justice that he hastily called a press conference just to get her off the air. The strategy backfired when the networks played back Mrs. Hamer's testimony that evening on prime time.)[44]

The FDP lobbying effort was clearly effective, and when it appeared that sufficient support existed in the Credentials Committee to bring the challenge to the convention floor, administration forces led by Senator Hubert Humphrey (who was eager to become the vice-presidential nominee) proposed a series of compromises. The final offer, to award FDP delegates Aaron Henry and Ed King at-large seats while welcoming the rest of the delegation as "honored guests" of the convention, won approval from the Credentials Committee. In a series of angry and exhausting meetings a solid majority of FDP delegates rejected the proposal, which would permit the state's all-white party to retain its official status. Nor were FDP delegates mollified by a pledge that in future conventions no state delegation could exclude blacks. Mrs. Hamer summed up the FDP's feelings simply and eloquently with the statement, "We didn't come all this way for no two seats!"[45]

The battle for representation in Atlantic City had two major consequences for the Mississippi movement. First, failure to seat the FDP embittered COFO veterans, who would regard Atlantic City as the ultimate betrayal by the liberal establishment. There they had seen white "champions" of the civil rights movement, including Hubert Humphrey and UAW president Walter Reuther, working round the clock to persuade fellow liberals in northern delegations to seat the Mississippi segregationists. FDP delegates directed much of their wrath toward their attorney, Joe Rauh, a leading spokesman for the Americans for Democratic Action and a confidant of Humphrey. Bob Moses and other COFO leaders believed then that Rauh had sold out FDP by making a secret deal with the Humphrey forces. But while Rauh favored the final compromise, he did attempt to delay a credentials subcommittee vote until he could place the proposal before an FDP caucus. Rauh was outmaneuvered here by a young attorney general from Minnesota named Walter Mondale, a Humphrey protege who, as chairman of the subcommittee, was taking his marching orders from the White House. Mondale forced an early vote on the compromise, then went on national television to announce that FDP had accepted it.[46] At that moment FDP strategists were meeting in a hotel room with Humphrey, unaware of the subcommittee action. As he watched Mondale's performance on live TV, an angry Bob Moses, believing FDP had been sandbagged, stormed out of the room, slamming the door on the next vice-president of the United States.[47]

FDP leaders knew that Lyndon Johnson was at work behind the scenes employing familiar arm-twisting tactics (such as threatening to withhold patronage from delegates supporting FDP), but for tactical reasons they decided not to go public with this information. What they did not know then was that the President had resorted to illegal means to gather intelligence on the FDP delegation. A 1976 Senate investigating committee, headed by Frank Church of Idaho, revealed that "approximately 30 special agents" of the FBI had provided the White House with "the most intimate details of the plans of individuals supporting the MFDP's challenge. . . ." Among "confidential techniques" employed by the FBI were a wiretap on Martin Luther King's hotel telephone and microphone surveillance of SNCC's Atlantic City headquarters.[48]

Although Lyndon Johnson kept a low profile throughout the debate (and did not even mention the FDP challenge in the section of his autobiography dealing with the convention) his presidential diary shows that in the days surrounding the convention he was obsessed by the challenge, directing a constant stream of telephone calls from the White House to Humphrey; to his top aides on the convention floor, Bill Moyers and Walter Jenkins; and to leading southern politicians, in particular Senator Eastland.[49] (Like John Kennedy, Lyndon Johnson preferred the company of professional politicians during times of racial crisis. There is no record of his having personal contact with anyone from FDP during the convention period.) Movement veterans left the convention embittered, having abandoned hope of any working relationship with the liberals who refused to take a meaningful stand against the forces of white supremacy in Mississippi.

The second major impact of Atlantic City was internal, marking the beginning of the end of the COFO partnership and the emergence of class conflict as a major destructive force in the Mississippi movement. Looking back on this experience, Bob Moses recently observed that "The thing that the movement had going for it . . . up until the convention was a unity among the black population about the program and goals. And that was shattered at the convention . . . the class thing I think came to a head at Atlantic City."[50] The problem began to surface earlier in the year, in the initial stages of FDP delegate selection. At first the traditional Negro leaders in Mississippi scoffed at the idea of the challenge, and refused to associate themselves with the effort. But when it became apparent that a 68-member delegation would go to Atlantic City, and that FDP was in fact winning support from influential northern Democrats, established ministers and well-to-do businessmen attempted to jump on the bandwagon.[51] SNCC and CORE organizers worked to block this move, for they wanted to get "as radical a delegation as you could . . . people who would stand up when they got to Atlantic City."[52] Thus at the FDP convention in Jackson activists took steps to make sure the delegation would be representative of the majority of the state's blacks, the rural poor. Although about a fifth of the delegation was comprised of traditional middle class leaders from the cities, important spokesmen such as the Reverend R.L.T. Smith, who was also the COFO treasurer, were excluded.[53]

The final FDP vote on the compromise at Atlantic City split along rural-urban and along class lines. Moses recalls that the delegates favoring the compromise were largely oriented toward the NAACP (the "more established people from the large cities"). Delegates from the rural areas voted against it.[54] The FDP debate over the compromise unleased tensions which had been repressed since the beginning of the movement. Fannie Lou

Hamer lashed out at Aaron Henry, who supported the compromise and left town after his delegation rejected it. Unita Blackwell, delegate from a small Delta community, angrily recalled a confrontation with a wealthy Meridian businessman:

> He had on a silk suit and he called us off and told us we've got to get this thing together. . . . Them people had not even been talking to us poor folks. . . . The big niggers talked to the big niggers, and the little folk, they couldn't talk to nobody except themselves. . . . They had decided they was going to take that compromise, but the little folks told them no, they wasn't going to take it and they meant business.[55]

Shortly after the convention SNCC field secretary Charles Sherrod reflected that "We could have accepted the compromise, called it a victory and gone back to Mississippi, carried on the shoulders of millions of Negroes across the country as their champions. But . . . we are what we are—hungry, beaten, unvictorious, jobless, homeless, but thankful to have the strength to fight."[56]

The returning FDP delegates would need all the strength they could muster, for in the weeks and months following Atlantic City they had to do battle on a number of fronts. In addition to white Mississippi Democrats, the list of ideological opponents ranged from conservative middle-class blacks determined to regain lost influence to embittered SNCC and CORE veterans who had lost faith in the system.

Atlantic City was also a turning point in the lives of COFO leaders Dave Dennis and Bob Moses. Dennis, once the most optimistic of the young organizers, had unfairly blamed himself in the deaths of the three civil rights workers, who were operating in his district. Now, at the end of the summer, his idealism shattered, Dennis left the state, having lost enthusiasm for "the nonviolent approach" he had championed for so long.[57] The experience was equally traumatic for Bob Moses, who had insisted on an interracial summer project and had spent countless hours in Atlantic City negotiating with the nation's liberal elite. Beginning in the fall of 1964 Moses turned his back on integra-

tionist politics and began to talk with blacks about setting up
their own parallel institutions: "Now why can't we set up our own
schools? Because when you come right down to it, why integrate
their schools? What Negroes really need to learn is how to be
organized to work on the society to change it." Moses then raised
the same question concerning the political system, proposing
that blacks organize their own government and then simply "de-
clare the other one no good."[58]

Such black nationalist talk frightened northern liberals who in
earlier days had identified with the young organizers in Mississippi. Now, in the fall of 1964, they began to employ the
strategy of divide and conquer, withdrawing support from black
radicals while encouraging the development of rival factions in
the state. Of particular concern to the liberals was the Freedom
Democratic Party, which they saw as an all-black group dominated by SNCC and obviously not subject to the discipline of the
national Democratic party. After a fact-finding tour of the South
in the fall of 1964, Americans for Democratic Action staff member
Curtis Gans recommended to his superiors that the ADA "use
whatever influence it has to urge SNCC to abandon the Freedom
Democratic orientation of its black belt party as being harmful to
the freedom and representation the Negroes seek." At the same
time, the ADA should push hard for voting rights legislation, for
"Quick granting of voting rights will mean quick recruitment by
the Democratic Party, which in turn will mean quick scuttling of
the Freedom Democratic parties and SNCC control." Finally,
Gans suggested that the ADA should "assist in a quiet freeze of
funds on these projects which do have a Freedom Democratic
Party orientation."[59] Here again was the Atlantic City mentality
at work: liberal Democrats know what is best for black people,
and blacks who refuse to accept enlightened white leadership
should be isolated. But for Bob Moses, "the liberals getting upset
at us was inevitable. We are raising fundamental questions about
how the poor sharecropper can achieve the Good Life, questions
that liberalism is incapable of answering."[60]

What liberal and conservative critics failed to realize (or preferred not to see) was that down in Mississippi the fledgling Freedom Democratic Party was struggling to steer a middle course between the SNCC radicals and NAACP conservatives. Under the leadership of Lawrence Guyot, a Tougaloo graduate and SNCC veteran, the FDP gave active support to (and supplied most of the votes for) the Johnson-Humphrey ticket in Mississippi. And as part of its effort to win recognition by the national Democratic Party, FDP mounted another challenge, this time to the seating of the state's congressional delegation. Some liberal Democrats supported this unsuccessful effort, but many others, including Lyndon Johnson, saw the move as just another example of FDP perfidy.

The Congressional challenge received public support from SNCC, FDP's parent organization, but privately SNCC was undergoing serious reappraisal of its mission in the South, particularly its future role in Mississippi. Many SNCC people were unhappy that FDP had chosen to continue to work within the political mainstream. Bob Moses believed that instead of the Congressional challenge, FDP should devote its energy to organizing around local issues. But he believed more strongly that local people should set their own agenda, and he would not impose his views on FDP. If he were to remain in Mississippi, Moses told SNCC's James Forman, he would have to do battle with Lawrence Guyot. This Moses refused to do, and soon permanently left the state.[61]

FDP's major internal opposition came from middle-class black Mississippians. During the early sixties COFO workers had cultivated a new group of black leaders who were often poor, without much formal education, and who had heretofore been ignored by the traditional black leadership.[62] Atlantic City had given legitimacy to people like Mrs. Hamer, Hartman Turnbow, and E. W. Steptoe, and the black middle class resented it. FDP leader Ed King observed that "suddenly a real class barrier developed the minute we got back from Atlantic City. The old Negro leadership class refused to work with the Freedom Party," and there developed "a kind of internal feuding within the Negro community from a displaced leadership class to restore itself and take the leadership over from a new class of leaders."[63] This opposition to the FDP had its organizational base in the NAACP.

As noted, although the NAACP national office had always distrusted the young radicals in COFO, local NAACP chapters had often worked closely with SNCC and CORE organizers. Freedom summer was no exception. But in the fall of 1964 complaints began to surface in communities where the NAACP was operating. The most common criticism was that after NAACP leaders welcomed the COFO workers into their communities and homes, COFO activists began to undermine the NAACP, charging that its leaders were "Uncle Toms" and urging young blacks in the community to renounce the old guard and ally with the young militants. Differences in lifestyle also separated the two groups. Older blacks were often offended at the summer volunteers' informal dress and alarmed by interracial courtships, particularly white women dating black men. While the national NAACP exploited these tensions, there is no denying that resentment against the young activists was building in NAACP chapters across the state, or that NAACP people had reason to be offended by the often insensitive and condescending attitudes of many COFO workers.[64]

By the winter of 1964–65 the Mississippi movement was in disarray. Many SNCC and CORE veterans left the state, battle weary and bitter. They left a vacuum which could not be filled by the scores of white volunteers who stayed on to work after freedom summer. Interracial tensions kept under control during the summer now exploded, further damaging morale and impeding movement activity in projects across the state. Local white hostility and acts of violence continued unabated, but the nation appeared to have lost interest in Mississippi, once again. The liberal press stepped up its attacks on black radicalism, and charges of communist infiltration of the movement filled the air. Given these external and internal pressures, the old coalition collapsed, ending symbolically in early 1965 when the NAACP pulled out of COFO and began looking for new allies in Mississippi.[65]

The last half of the decade would see continued black protest, and at times the old alliances would be temporarily restored, for the real enemy had not changed. But in 1966 COFO disbanded, and the Freedom Democratic Party, still attempting to be recognized as an independent political force within the Democratic Party, was finding it increasingly difficult to overcome the opposition of both the Johnson administration and the established NAACP leadership.[66] Perhaps the best example of the changes occuring in the Mississippi movement was the emergence of Charles Evers as the new national symbol of the freedom struggle in the state. Combining charismatic appeal with old-fashioned political wheeling and dealing, Evers built his own political empire, and was bitterly resented by FDP activists. That Evers had won the endorsement of many former friends of COFO in the North did not make him any less objectionable!

In the mid-1960s a new face had appeared on the political scene, that of the white Mississippi moderate. Centered in the Delta, this small group of professionals included men like attorneys Douglas Wynn and Wesley Watkins, planter Oscar Carr, and editor Hodding Carter III. Equally opposed to the Eastland wing of the Democratic Party and to the Freedom Democratic Party and its supporters, this new faction backed the Johnson administration in war and peace and soon made influential friends in Washington.[67] At the same time the FDP was trying to gain credibility with national party leaders, Vice-President Humphrey was meeting quietly with Doug Wynn and other white moderates to discuss the "problems of the Democratic Party in Mississippi."[68]

This new faction obtained an organizational base in the Mississippi Young Democrats (after a bitter battle with an FDP-backed group over the state charter), and with White House assistance won control over a large chunk of the poverty program

and its political patronage. All that remained was for them to
establish formal ties with the old-line NAACP stalwarts, including
Aaron Henry and Charles Evers, for the new alliance to become
complete. FDP worked desperately to defeat this coalition, but
their resources were dwindling and the opposition too powerful.
In the summer of 1968 the Freedom Democrats made a reluctant
peace with the Carter-Henry group to become part of the Loyalist challenge to the regular state delegation at the Democratic
National Convention.

When the Loyalists were in fact seated at the stormy Chicago
convention the national media trumpeted the victory as a triumph for the civil rights forces in Mississippi, and in a sense it
was. But a different breed had captured the movement banner:
urban, educated, and affluent, these new leaders had their own
agenda. Few of them were organizers, and they had little contact
with the black masses, for whom they professed to speak. They
were a far cry from the band of brothers and sisters who had
"challenged America" on the back roads of Mississippi, in search
of the Beloved Community.

Looking back on the civil rights movement in Mississippi from
the vantage point of two decades, two points stand clear. First,
the movement accomplished many of the goals set during its first
wave in the 1950s. The Jim Crow society which Medgar Evers
condemned so forcefully shortly before his martyrdom now be-
longs to the dustbin of history. Blacks won the vote and the right
to organize their communities. In so doing they changed the
complexion of Mississippi politics. The victories were real, they
are important, and we should not demean them, for they were
purchased with the blood and sacrifice of thousands of extraordinary black Mississippians.

And yet it is also true that the vision of a Fannie Lou Hamer
remains just that, yet another dream deferred. Twenty years ago
Bob Moses spoke for the movement when he raised "fundamental questions about how the poor sharecropper can achieve the
Good Life," questions which still haunt us today. But in attempt-

ing to understand those forces which have resisted that "Third
Reconstruction," one which would finally address the ongoing
problems of poverty and powerlessness among hundreds of thousands of Mississippians, black and white, we need to look beyond
the civil rights movement and Mississippi to the heart and soul of
this nation itself.

Commentary / Neil R. McMillen

Professor Dittmer has contributed importantly to a story told in
part by others—notably, to name but four writers, by Cleveland
Sellers and John Salter, in their respective autobiographies, *The
River of No Return* and *Jackson, Mississippi;* by Steven Lawson,
in two wide-ranging works, *Black Ballots* and more recently
Pursuit of Power; and by Clayborne Carson, in his book *In
Struggle: SNCC and the Black Awakening of the 1960s.* Concentrating exclusively on civil rights activism in one state, Dittmer has mined the Mississippi sources intensively. His
documentation for this paper suggests the solid base upon which
his book will rest: the oral history projects of Howard University
and the presidential libraries, and his own extensive interviews
with movement activists and other principals; the papers of the
NAACP, the Americans for Democratic Action, and the administrations of Kennedy and Johnson; collections in private, state,
and university archives.

The history of the Mississippi Movement—in its broadest con-
tours—is, of course, not unfamiliar. Dittmer, if only in passing,
mentions the major events of the era: from the NAACP school-
desegregation petitions and early voter registration drives; to the
advent of SNCC, the formation of COFO, and the alienation engen-
dered by the cautious federalism and inaction of the Kennedy-
Johnson administrations; to Freedom Summer and the MFDP, the
subsequent collapse of the civil rights coalition,and the ultimate
triumph of the Loyalist faction of the state Democratic party.

In the process, he adds a welcome measure of clarity to a

complicated era by dividing Movement history, if at times only by implication, into three relatively distinct phases (two of which he calls waves)—the first ending with the bankruptcy of NAACP tactics in the late 1950s; the second beginning after 1960 through the impatience of a new and more militant generation of black Mississippians and the arrival of the "emergent civil rights organizations;" and the third coming after the MFDP challenge to the regular Democrats in 1964, after the shattering of Movement unity, with the rise of what might be called a new centrist coalition of young white moderates and old-line black stalwarts. Of course, he sees continuity, too. But unlike Carson, he sees more continuity between the first and second waves than between the second and third.

This periodization is welcome and useful. But the primary value of the paper lies in the analysis of changing leadership patterns in Mississippi. And it lies in the new and highly suggestive light Dittmer casts on the disintegration of Movement unity and inter-organizational harmony in Mississippi. Others have described tensions that ultimately contributed to the Movement's fragmentation. During the 1960s, black Mississippians, as Charles Evers' autobiography reminds us, invested their hopes in a unified civil rights front but could hardly ignore the divisions that separated what they called "been here" and "come here" activists—or, to view the dichotomy as the Citizens' Council did, between native black malcontents and the "outside agitators" of both races. Cleveland Sellers has described the conflicts within SNCC between "philosophers, anarchists, floaters, and freedom high niggers" on the one hand and "hardliners" on the other, between those he thought to be impractical visionaries and those he thought to be disciplined activists. John Salter has movingly recounted the organizational jealousies that led officers of the national NAACP into a tacit conspiracy, a profoundly incongruous alliance of convenience, with the Kennedy administration and, apparently, with local white authorities against the grassroots movement he led in Jackson. Reese Cleghorn and Pat Watters, and most systematically Clayborne Carson, have described both the tactical disagreements and the color conflicts that divided nationalist from integrationist and set militant black against liberal white in a movement initially dedicated to nonviolence and biracialism. Dittmer has effectively drawn on these themes; and more tellingly than any other history of the Mississippi Movement, he has developed in some detail yet another, that of class conflict, the conflict between the state's relatively advantaged traditional black leadership class and its black masses, between what Unita Blackwell chose to call Mississippi's "big niggers" and its "little folk." Bill Chafe's important Greensboro study shows that such conflict was not unique to Mississippi. Yet one could argue that—because Mississippi was in an oppressive class by itself, and because its traditional black leadership was often so cautious and conservative—that class conflict was perhaps more disruptive to the Movement than it might have been in other states.

In a sense, what Dittmer offers is a partial response to Clay Carson's appeal for greater scholarly emphasis on local movements and local leadership. In describing changing leadership patterns at the state and local level he draws our attention to a compound revolution—to what a Carl Becker would call a "revolution within a revolution"—the one, an external revolution, the revolt of black Mississippians against their white oppressors; the other, an internal revolution, the revolt of black "have nots" against their former leaders, the black "haves." Viewed from the perspective of the old middle-class, the internal revolution resulted in a loss of deference, a status revolution, the displacement of traditional elites once thought to be the natural leaders of their people by the people themselves.

What Professor Dittmer has presented here is a valuable insight that deepens our understanding of one of the major social movements of our time. Given the significance of his argument, it seems almost churlish to ask for more. Yet because he has elected to focus on a relatively narrow subject, the internal politics of the

Movement, one wishes that his paper were some how tighter, that he had wrapped together more securely the several strands of his thesis, that he had perhaps said less about the larger context, perhaps less even about Movement interaction with the Kennedy administration, so that he could have developed his central insight more fully. If this valuable paper has a flaw, then, it is technical rather than substantive and it is to be found in the fact that its conceptual center is sometimes obscured by the telling of the larger story of the freedom struggle in Mississippi. That flaw, if flaw it is, pales, however, in light of the contribution.

The paper, in sum, sharpens our appetite for the book it foreshadows. One wants to know about the important role played by black women in the second-wave period, a role Dittmer mentions only in passing. In light of the wide currency given Stokely Carmichael's regrettably flip and chauvanistic comment about the "proper position" of women in the struggle, Dittmer's investigations into this topic should serve as a useful corrective to the conventional wisdom. One wants to know a good deal more about the local, indigenous, independent movements, the grass-roots movements that operated in such cities as Jackson, Clarksdale, Greenwood, and Hattiesburg, One wants to know about the role of pre-existing black community institutions within these local movements. One wants to know how these were reshaped by the movements, how they were altered by the freedom struggle. One looks forward to learning more about the major voter registration campaigns in McComb and Greenwood. Not least of all one wants to know more about the impact, the place of the Mississippi Movement in the context of the larger black revolution. No doubt, as Steven Lawson had recently noted, Mississippi in the early 1960s was the "laboratory in which the civil rights movement displayed its most creative energies." Because that is true, the appearance of Dittmer's book is awaited all the more impatiently.

Federal Law and the Courts in the Civil Rights Movement

CHARLES V. HAMILTON

What came to be known in the United States as the civil rights movement—from the early 20th century to the late 1960s—was first and foremost a movement to end *de jure* segregation in the country. Let this presentation begin with an unambiguous conclusion: that movement was successful. Blatant, overt laws requiring segregation of the races were declared unconstitutional, and laws denying and impeding the right of black Americans to vote were ended. In this sense, the civil rights movement that most people joined (or opposed) was won.

To be sure, there were always efforts at overcoming *de facto* segregation and discrimination. And equally clear, these efforts continue, but the first, fundamental goal of the civil rights movement—to square the statutes with the constitution—was achieved. Segregation effects and discriminatory practices remain, but this is the next, important phase of the struggle—Civil Rights II, if you will. But Civil Rights I is over, and it was successful.

This paper will focus on the role of the federal courts and federal laws in achieving that momentous victory. It will address the following proposition:

Changes in the civil rights of blacks resulted not just from protests and demonstrations carried out by individuals and organizations at the local level, but also from laws implemented by Congress and from the actions of federal judges.

97

The intent of this paper is to analyze the approach and impact of court decisions and laws. It is organized in four parts. First, the necessity and rationale for a judicio-legislative strategy. Second, the evolution of that strategy, covering voting rights cases, education, public accommodations, and the civil rights and voting rights laws. Here it will discuss the courts' willingness to overrule the efforts of subterfuge practiced by local segregationists. Third, the inter-relationship of laws and protests. Fourth, a concluding section discussing the movement from "rights to resources," and the issues law and courts will be called upon to address. Dealing with the last set of problems will point out the differences between the earlier civil rights movement and the current phase, as well as the limitations of and opportunities for a judicio-legislative strategy.

I.

Two basic reasons dictated an emphasis on the legal attack on—as opposed to an essentially "political" approach to—segregation. First, racial segregation was embedded in the state laws and, since *Plessy* v. *Ferguson* (1896), sanctioned by the U.S. Supreme Court as consistent with constitutional principles. This meant, at the outset, that the *legal* legitimacy of segregation had to be confronted. Next, given the objective political circumstances, neither the elected political officials at the state/local levels nor at the congressional/presidential level were amenable to the demands of the civil rights proponents. Blacks for the most part could not vote in the southern states where *de jure* segregation was reality and, therefore, they had virtually no influence at that level. In addition, national decision-makers (congressional and executive) were not responsive. Over twenty years of attempting to pass anti-lynching legislation (Dyer anti-lynching bill) were testimony enough in regard to the intransigence of Congress. That body was composed of powerful southern legislators who were obviously not going to be sympathetic to demands to dismantle a racially segregated system. They owed their *political* existence to the *legal* status quo, and there was no reason to suspect they would be prone to alter that base. Likewise, their positions in Congress afforded them added clout. Because of seniority, they occupied some important committee chairmanships. Their support for other legislation was needed in the trading and bargaining that inevitably took place in a legislative body. Plus, the rule of unlimited debate (filibuster) was enormously useful in blocking bills aimed at effective congressional action.

The executive branch was no more responsive. Whatever Woodrow Wilson's views were about "making the world safe for democracy," he apparently had no qualms about encouraging Washington, D.C., to become even more segregated. Even Franklin D. Roosevelt is not noted for a liberal posture on civil rights. For her time, perhaps, *Mrs.* Roosevelt. But not the President. And he had to be pressured and threatened with a mass march on Washington in 1940 by A. Philip Randolph before he issued an Executive Order (8802) establishing the President's Committee on Fair Employment Practices.

These halting, hesitant and all-too-reluctant responses from Congress and the executive branch led many civil rights proponents to conclude that the most viable route lay in a judicial direction. One that was aimed at attacking the fundamental *constitutional* basis for *de jure* segregation. The courts, therefore, became critical focal points. And this meant, of course, the *federal* courts, which, in turn, obviously and ultimately meant the highest court in the land—the United States Supreme Court.

II.

One of the major contributions of the federal courts was the willingness of some judges to overrule the efforts at subterfuge practiced by local segregationists in the attempt to maintain the status quo.

Largely because most of the targets of the earlier civil rights movement involved *de jure* segregation, the remedies could be framed in "color-blind" terms. Battles were fought to permit blacks to vote on the same basis as other citizens were permitted to do so; "white" and "colored" signs stood as clear reminders of an officially sanctioned segregated society; dual school systems in the South were legally required, and in the North, normally expected. One could, therefore, mount campaigns to dismantle the segregated system by using "color-blind" language. The goals could be achieved in the name of *individual* rights, although a group (particularly blacks) was the specific focus of concern. There was no conflict, essentially, between civil libertarians and civil righters. In fact, the two functioned quite comfortably together. This was a partnership that assumed a common interest in protecting certain basic principles of egalitarianism: among these being a commitment to selection on the basis of merit, not ascription, with primary emphasis on individual liberty. David Apter calls this the "secular libertarian model," which is "the classic liberal picture of a political community."[1] He suggests:

> The citizens are politically equal, as in the concept of one man, one vote. Power and loyalty are constantly being exchanged for benefits and privileges. The voting mechanism is the equivalent of the market. Preferences are rationally registered by the citizens as choices in the political arena. In this model, the primary value is liberty.[2]

The earlier civil rights movement had no need to challenge these "principles of legitimacy" as long as the goals dealt with blatant discrimination against a *group*. Thus, that movement could call for *individual* rights of equal treatment and be perfectly consistent with secular libertarianism. This conceptual articulation of the matter will reappear in the last section of this paper. For now, it is necessary to turn to the very important role played by some judges and how they used their positions to deal with the *reality* of racism, not the rhetoric of egalitarianism. For purposes of this conference and paper, this is likely the most important observation to be made.

While color-blind goals characterized the earlier civil rights movement, it was also the case that care had to be taken against subtle efforts by segregationists to maintain the status quo while presenting the pretense of being color-blind. In attempting to resist the right of blacks to vote, for example, some devices were concocted that left the discriminatory franchise system intact without alluding to race. Whether the method was the "grandfather clause,"[3] the "white primary,"[4] or action by resistent registrars,[5] the federal courts ultimately disallowed the evasive, ostensibly color-blind tactics.

One of the surest devices for disfranchising black citizens was the grandfather clause. This method had many variations from state to state,[6] but the fundamental effect was to deny the vote to those persons in the state who could not pass a stiff registration test. Those failing this examination would be permitted to vote, nonetheless, if they or their ancestors had voted in the state or some other jurisdiction before a certain specified date—1860, 1866, or 1870. Since blacks usually were slaves in the southern states or could not show that they personally had voted before the particular year, they were prohibited from voting. Oklahoma had amended its constitution, but the requirement did not apply to people whose ancestors had been entitled to vote on January 1, 1866. A case challenging the 1866 standard worked its way up through the courts, until the Supreme Court said that the state's provision, harking back to conditions that existed before the passage of the Fifteenth Amendment, had made these conditions "the basis of the right to suffrage conferred in direct and positive disregard of the Fifteenth Amendment."[7]

After a series of cases dealing with the states' efforts to restrict primary elections to white voters, the federal courts ultimately disallowed attempts to devolve the regulation of primaries onto "private" agencies. The Democratic party of South Carolina had adopted rules under which control of the primaries in that state was vested in the clubs to which blacks were not admitted to membership, and voting in the primaries was conditioned on the voter's taking an oath that he or she believed in the social and educational separation of the races and was "opposed to the proposed federal so-called FEPC law."

Judge John J. Parker then ruled that the state or the political party could not do indirectly what the U.S. constitution and the courts had prohibited them from doing directly, that even though the election laws did not mention race specifically, they could not be administered to discriminate against blacks. In this instance, the Democratic party of South Carolina was in fact taking over and performing

> a vital part of its [state's] electoral machinery. . . . *Courts of equity are neither blind nor impotent.* They exercise their injunctive power to strike directly at the source of evil which they are seeking to prevent. The evil here is racial discrimination which bars negro voters from any effective participation in the government of their state; and when it appears that this discrimination is practiced through rules of a party which controls the primary elections, these must be enjoined just as any other practice which threatens to corrupt elections or direct them from their constitutional purpose.[8] [emphasis added.]

It was clear that the federal courts were not going to be easily misled by state legislatures or allegedly private organizations performing state functions. But it was also clear that the forces for resisting change were not easily deterred in their goals. Boards of registrators had considerable leeway in administering voter-registration tests. They could be, ostensibly, color-blind but, in fact, perform their duties in such discriminatory ways as to effectively preclude the registration of significant numbers of black applicants. Increased attention turned to literacy tests, voucher systems, purges, and various methods of slowing the registration process. V. O. Key wrote in 1949:

> No matter from what direction one looks at it, the southern literacy test is a fraud and nothing more. The simple fact seems to be that the constitutionally prescribed test of ability to read and write a section of the constitution is rarely administered to whites. It is applied chiefly to Negroes and not always to them.

When Negroes are tested on their ability to read and write, only in exceptional instances is the test administered fairly. Insofar as is known, no southern registration official has utilized an objective test of literacy.[9]

But with the enactment of the civil rights laws of 1957 and 1960 (and, subsequently, 1964 and 1965), these obstacles were slowly overcome. In the early 1960s, seeing that they must move toward the appearance, if not the actuality, of a color-blind voter-registration system, some southern registrars began applying a "single standard" for all applicants.

In Bullock County, Alabama, the registrars adopted very strict standards which they applied to white and black applicants alike. The U.S. Department of Justice was able to convince Federal District Court Judge Frank M. Johnson, Jr., that this was a "constitutionally suspect" procedure, because "to require future applicants, white and Negro, to complete their applications with technical precision . . . amounts to a freezing of the status quo. And the effect is the practical disfranchisement of almost 99 percent of the unregistered Negroes, while only about 5 percent of the whites remain unregistered." Neither was Judge Johnson persuaded that the registrars in Montgomery County, Alabama, were entirely color-blind in administering the single standard of technical precision. After February 1961, the Montgomery Board of Registrars instituted registration standards to require a perfect application. Very strict requirements were put on white and black applicants alike. (This was similar to the Bullock County single-standard freezing tactic.) Yet registrars continued to give assistance to whites. Judge Johnson made a careful study of the applications of whites accepted and of the blacks rejected during a certain period. In a two-year period from 1958 to 1960, approximately 600 black applicants were rejected for failure to sign the oath on page three of the four-page questionnaire, although the oath was administered orally and was to be signed in the presence of the registrar. "Yet," Judge Johnson stated, "the registrars let the Negroes walk out of the office without calling the ommission of their attention. Such a practice by the Board evidences bad faith and leads to the inevitable conclusion that such a device was used by them for deception." Exhibits showed that hundreds of white applicants had x's, check marks, dots, and dashes on the oath line of the application form. Judge Johnson concluded from this that "they were made by the registrars and made for the purpose of showing the white applicants where to sign."

What was, then, in appearance a color-blind process was in fact quite the opposite. And some federal judges refused to ignore the fact in their decision making. They found that they had to be candid and quite specific in what they would and would not accept as color-blind practices. It is difficult to overstate the important of the judiciary's willingness in those times to go, in a sense, to the heart of the matter. On more than a few occasions judges refused to be sidetracked or put off by spurious arguments, delaying tactics, or questionable practices. It would be inaccurate to conclude, however, that this was the case in every instance. If Judge Johnson in Alabama was an example of judicial aggressiveness, then surely federal judges Harold Cox and Claude Clayton in Mississippi were quite the contrary. They granted interminable delays and issued very weak enforcement orders. They commented on the generally lower level of education of blacks, and they were openly concerned about potential bloc voting among blacks.

In one case, *U.S. v. Lynd* (301 Fed. 2d 818) (1962), the evidence showed that white applicants were registered by the registrar's deputies while every black applicant had to be registered personally by the registrar, a Mr. Theron C. Lynd. The justification was that the deputies were "apprehensive" about registering blacks. The only testimony regarding the cause of the apprehension was that on one occasion an unidentified black man had asked the woman deputy a "personal question." (He had asked her: "How long I had been there and didn't he know me and didn't I remember him and one thing and another.") On another occasion, a black woman fumbled in her handbag while waiting

for the registrar, left the office, and returned with a black man.
When the Justice Department lawyers asked Judge Cox to end
the practice of requiring all blacks to be registered personally by
Lynd (which, of course, would slow up the process) Judge Cox
refused, stating:

> I think the colored people brought that on themselves. I am
> thoroughly familiar with some of the conduct of some of our
> colored gentry, and I am not surprised at Mr. Lynd's reaction to
> what he did. You people up North don't understand what he
> was talking about and I think he did just exactly right in taking
> those things on himself. He said he couldn't afford any male
> help and he used girls in there and those girls didn't want to be
> subjected to that kind of influence and that is understandable.
> Otherwise I think that he certainly did need a good explana-
> tion. [10]

Essentially, people like Cox and Clayton simply had to be
overruled by the appellate court or forced through threats of
mandamus actions to move the cases. On balance, however, the
southern district court judges—aggressively or reluctantly—performed the judicial functions expected of them.

It is also accurate to suggest that the mixed record of judicial
enforcement was significant in arguing the need for stronger civil
rights legislation which came in 1964 and 1965. Many people
were becoming convinced that even where the Judge Johnsons
and Judge Wisdoms (5th Circuit) and some others were willing
and ready to do what they could within the limits of legal evidence and rules of procedure, the situation called for more effective laws with greater possibility for executive action and
enforcement.

Civil rights proponents have long been aware of the potential
and actual usefulness of the federal courts to their struggle.
Indeed, the NAACP lawyers who began in the 1930s to fashion
legal strategies to overturn segregation in education (first, higher
education, then elementary and secondary) understood this.
Genna Rae McNeil, in her book, *Groundwork, Charles
Hamilton Houston and the Struggle for Civil Rights*, (1983) de-

scribes the work and thinking of one of the architects of the modern legal civil rights strategy:

> In the Court a black man could "compel a white man to listen," and reforms could be forced when blacks had no chance through politics. So convinced was Charles Houston of the correctness of his theory of social engineering and its potential with respect to prompting a nondiscriminatory interpretation of the Constitution or federal statutes that he taught students a lawyer was "either a social engineer or a parasite on society."

> In its reliance on resort to courts for gaining recognition of their constitutional rights, social engineering was consistent with the traditional faith of African-Americans in the possibility of changing their subordinate status not only through resistance but also through protests and appeals based on the expressed fundamental principles of the U.S. government. The influence of social engineering on the black jurisprudential matrix was significant and novel in its exposition of the duties of black American lawyers and its presentation of the rationale for use of the law by blacks."

There was no blind faith in "the law" as such. The lawyers knew quite well the legal precedents they had to overcome, the embedded ideology of racism frequently reflected in previous court decisions.[12] The admonitions of Taney in the Dred Scott decision, and the language of the Supreme Court in *Plessy* v. *Ferguson* were not unknown to them.

Indeed, McNeil chronicled Houston's careful legal approach:

> In planning his activity, he took into account *stare decisis*, judicial self-restraint, the step-by-step process and the requirement of reasonable predictability of legal consequences. The result was a three-pronged strategy: selecting cases that presented clear legal issues and building strong records in those cases; overturning negative legal decisions by invalidating gradually or attacking directly the controlling precedents, and developing a sustaining community or mass interest in each case.[13]

The legal strategy, in other words, gave the civil rights movement assets it did not have in other arenas. Sound arguments could be presented in a court of law, when those arguments might not be relevant in the halls of Congress. Careful constitutional lawyers at the time were as (if not more) important as precinct captains. Blacks had to go where their available weapons took them—to court, not to the polling booths. It would take legal action to unlock the voting booths, the segregated school rooms, the segregated lunch counters, the segregated interstate travel facilities.

And the legal strategists could argue for their interpretation of a more enlightened approach to the constitution. They knew that if they stood on legal precedent alone, they would likely not prevail. Thus, it was important to push for an "experiential" interpretation of the constitution. This involved seeing the law in terms of existing circumstances, analyzing the cases in light of present conditions. It was important that Charles Warren's observation be understood:

> The Court is not an organism dissociated from the conditions and history of the times in which it exists. It does not formulate and deliver its opinions in a legal vacuum. Its judges are not abstract and impersonal oracles, but are men whose views are necessarily, though by no conscious intent, affected by inheritance, education and environment and by the impact of history past and present. . . .[14]

And in this vein, civil rights lawyers shared the assessment of no less a prominent jurist and scholar, Oliver Wendell Holmes, who wrote:

> The life of the law has not been logic; it has been experience. The felt necessities of the time, the prevalent moral and political theories, institutions of public policy, avowed or unconscious, even the prejudices which judges share with their fellow-men, have had a good deal more to do than the syllogism in determining the rules by which men should be governed.[15]

This approach had its advantages and disadvantages, of course. One Court's (or judge's) interpretation of the "felt necessities of the time" might differ from that of another. Certainly, Judge Cox's "prejudices" differed from those of Judge Johnson's. One had to be careful in relying on this "experiential" approach. In fact, some critics have argued, it *is* social engineering and not really "law" at all. This is sociology and psychology—not "law." But the civil rights "social engineer" lawyers were prepared to take their chances—in the context of events unfolding in the 1940s and 1950s—indeed, into the 1960s. The culmination of their court-room efforts came in 1954 in *Brown v. Board*. There, Chief Justice Earl Warren clearly articulated an "experiential"[16] approach in his opinion for the majority. He wrote:

> In approaching this problem, we cannot turn the clock back to 1868 when the [14th] Amendment was adopted, or even to 1896 when *Plessy* v. *Ferguson* was written. We must consider public education in the light of its full development and its present place in American life throughout the nation. Only in this way can it be determined if segregation in public schools deprives these plaintiffs of the equal protection of the laws.[17]

These views coincided completely with those of civil rights advocates intent on ending racial segregation. And to have them pronounced by the highest court in the land in a unanimous opinion gave legitimacy—moral as well as legal—and credibility to the civil rights goals. The Supreme Court was seen as a definite ally, notwithstanding what might happen in the lower courts.

But even at the district court level, there was tremendous feeling of comfort on the part of civil rights activists. It must be understood that in the context of the years of the 1950s into the 1960s, local, southern state forums (with some exceptions such as Frank Johnson) were not perceived as friendly environments. These forums had virtually no legitimacy in the eyes of civil rights proponents. Therefore, at all times the focus was on getting the *national* government involved. This meant the federal courts surely, and it meant pressing for congressional action.[17]

An added appreciation of this point comes from reading the perceptive comments of Martin Luther King, Jr., describing the experiences of the Montgomery bus boycott activists in the late 1950s:

The intransigence of the city commission, the crudeness of the "get-touch" policy, and the viciousness of the recent bombings convinced us all that an attack must be made upon bus segregation itself. Accordingly, a suit was filed in the United States Federal District Court, asking for an end of bus segregation on the grounds that it was contrary to the Fourteenth Amendment. The court was also asked to stop the city commissioners from violating the civil rights of Negro motorists and pedestrians.

The hearing was set for May 11, 1956, before a three-judge federal court panel. *It was a great relief to be in a federal court. Here the atmosphere of justice prevailed.* No one can understand the feeling that comes to a Southern Negro on entering a federal court unless he sees with his own eyes and feels with his own soul the tragic sabotage of justice in the city and state courts of the South. The Negro goes into these courts knowing that the cards are stacked against him. Here he is virtually certain to face a prejudiced jury or a biased judge, and is openly robbed with little hope or redress. *But the Southern Negro goes into the federal court with the feeling that he has an honest chance of justice before the law.*[18] [emphasis added.]

This is an important observation. Blacks and many whites were keenly aware of the subterfuge practiced by southern officials. The laws and practices of segregation were blatant, but there were many devious and technical ways to protect and maintain those circumstances. If blacks relied solely on the established local institutions for redress of grievances, there was little likelihood of success. Thus, it was absolutely crucial that forces beyond the state and local governments intervene. And this meant turning to the national government.

When this was done, however, there was the inevitable argument of "federalism." This manifested itself in the perennial cry of "states' rights," and the claim would not be dismissed summarily.

When he was Assistant Attorney General, Civil Rights Division, Burke Marshall delivered a lecture in 1964 at Columbia University. His comments captured the constitutional *and social* dilemma of the times regarding federalism and the enforcement of civil rights. His words are reflective precisely of the issues raised. Marshall concluded:

> It does not accomplish much to generalize about the urgency and dimensions of the racial problem. But it is necessary to be realistic about the limitations on the power of the federal government to eliminate racial discrimination by simple law enforcement. These limitations are reflected in the experience of the Department of Justice in the last few years, since it was first given any responsibility or authority in this field. Certainly they are relevant to future law enforcement once new civil rights legislation is passed. They derive from two aspects of the federal system: the control of state institutions over normally routine decisions affecting the daily lives of all citizens and the traditional and constitutional reluctance of the federal courts to intrude. When this control is exercised without consideration of race problems, any federal-state conflicts are sporadic and haphazard. But when the issue of segregation is involved, the controls make it everlastingly tedious, sometimes seemingly impossible, to superimpose federal standards upon the administration practiced by local institutions of government.
>
> The danger is in the people directly affected. There exists an immense ignorance, apparently untouched by the curricula of the best universities, of the consequences of the federal system. When a violation of federal law occurs, most of those participating in civil rights work in the South (and there are thousands) think an arrest should be made by a federal officer. If there is none, and imprisonment or violence results, it is federal law and the federal government that is blamed.[19]

And then, taking his cue apparently from the academic locale of his presentation, Marshall admonished:

> This has led in the past three years to the greatest single source of frustration with and misunderstanding of the federal government, particularly among young people. They cannot understand federal inaction in the face of what they consider, often quite correctly, as official wholesale local interference with the exercise of federal constitutional rights. Apparently their schools and universities have not taught them much about the

working of the federal system. In their eyes the matter is simple. Local authorities are depriving certain people of their federal rights, often in the presence of federal officials from the Justice Department. Persons doing this should be protected.

What is wrong with this analysis? Is the federal government simply failing to meet a clear responsibility for enforcing federal law?

The question embraces all the deepest complexities of the federal system. It is surrounded by some basic constitutional notions which have worked, and worked well, in other contexts, preserving the dilution of powers intended by the framers of the Constitution, and at the same time protecting individuals against deprivation of their freedom. [20]

In one sense, Marshall was quite correct: In their (civil rights protesters') eyes the matter *was* simple. But were they "ignorant" of the "consequences of the federal system"? Had their schools failed to teach them "about the working of the federal system"? Or was something else taking place during those turbulent years of protest, politics, and American law? In fact, were not the protesters challenging the very foundation of American civil society and putting the test to political structures that, indeed, "worked well in other contexts" but witnessed "official wholesale local interference with the exercise of federal constitutional rights"? This was not a matter of lack of knowledge of or understanding of federalism. It was fundamental disagreement with its operation.

The protesters understood all too well. They were putting hard constitutional questions to the polity, requiring public choices between individual liberty and preference for political structures.

In the nature of things, such basic questions could best be answered in the law. Political protest could stir the ground and it did. But if governing institutions were to maintain their credibility with those who (remember Burke Marshall's own words: "often quite correctly") saw their constitutional rights being violated, then decisions had to be taken, choices made. It was a matter, ultimately of "legitimacy," and "the law" was seen as the best mechanism to use.

III.

If the civil rights movement could not rely on "the law" (that is, *its* interpretation of the meaning of the 14th and 15th amendments to the constitution) and the courts and the *federal* government to pass and enforce legislation, it had very little going for it. Protest could stir the conscience, create concern, focus attention. But ultimately, court decisions had to be rendered, executive decrees issued, legislation passed There had to be concrete outputs giving substance to the demands. Persuasion had to be codified into rules for future behavior, defining new relationships, spelling out new meanings of rights and obligations, limits and liabilities. *De jure* segregation had to give way to *de jure* desegregation.

But in the process of pursuing their cause, civil rights protesters were not always successful in the highest court of the land. In the spring of 1963, Martin Luther King, Jr., and his associates planned nonviolent demonstrations in Birmingham, Alabama, protesting racial segregation and discrimination in that city. They sought and were denied a permit to do so from the city Commissioner of Public Safety. The denial was based on a city ordinance giving the official authority to refuse permission if, in his judgment, the demonstration "threatened the safety, peace and tranquility of the city," and placed "an undue burden and strain upon the manpower of the Police Department." King and others planned to demonstrate nonetheless, and the city received a temporary injunction against them. The protesters disobeyed the injunction on the grounds that it was unconstitutionally vague, restrained free speech, and had been previously administered in an arbitrary and discriminatory manner. They refused also to take their case to the state courts, declaring, interestingly, in a press conference: "[they] had respect for the Federal Courts, or Federal injunctions, but in the past the state courts had favored local law enforcement. . . ."

The U.S. Supreme Court in *Walker* v. *Birmingham*[21] ruled against the civil rights groups, telling them they should have

challenged the injunction in the Alabama courts. "The petitioners gave absolutely no explanation of why they did not make
some application to the state court. . . ." "It cannot be presumed
that the Alabama courts would have ignored the petitioners'
constitutional claims. . . . One may sympathize with the petitioners' impatient commitment to their cause. But respect for
judicial process is a small price to pay for the civilizing hand of
law, which alone can give abiding meaning to constitutional freedom."

Four justices (Warren, Brennan, Fortas, Douglas) dissented.
They believed that, in fact, the city had no intention of issuing a
permit. Warren wrote: "I dissent because I do not believe that the
fundamental protections of the Constitution were meant to be so
easily evaded, or that 'the civilizing hand of law' would be ham-
pered in the slightest by enforcing the First Amendment in this
case." In addition:

> When local officials are given totally unfettered discretion to
> decide whether a proposed demonstration is consistent with
> 'public welfare, peace, safety, health, decency, good order,
> morals or convenience,' . . . they are invited to act as censors
> over the views that may be presented to the public. The
> unconstitutionality of the ordinance is compounded, of course,
> when there is convincing evidence that the officials have in fact
> used their power to deny permits to organizations whose views
> they dislike. The record in this case hardly suggests that Com-
> missioner Connor and the other city officials were motivated in
> prohibiting civil rights picketing only by their overwhelming
> concern for particular traffic problems. Petitioners were given
> to understand that under no circumstances would they be
> permitted to demonstrate in Birmingham, not that a demon-
> stration would be approved if a time and place were selected
> that would minimize the traffic difficulties.

A few years later, the U.S. Supreme Court in *Carroll* v. *President and Commissioners of Princess Anne*[22] decided that injunctions restraining exercise of First Amendment rights may not be
issued ex parte if the defendants can be notified and granted a
hearing. This did not deal with the basic issue of civil disobe-

dience, but in 1969 in *Shuttlesworth* v. *Birmingham*[23] the Supreme Court declared unconstitutional the Birmingham ordinance which was the basis of the *Walker* decision.

The important observation is that even though the civil rights movement did not always win in the federal courts (even the Supreme Court) at the height of the movement—Martin Luther King, Jr., and others, in fact, went to jail—the Court provided a creditable forum in which to make an argument. The dissents in *Walker* were valuable at the time precisely because they cut through the pretense of impartiality and objectivity of law enforcement on the part of state and local officials. The Supreme Court dissenters were saying exactly what lower federal courts had been saying back in the 1940s regarding the state subterfuge in white primary cases. Indeed, what Judge Frank M. Johnson was telling the voter-registrars in those Alabama counties—in other words: stop the nonsense; stop pretending to be fair and square; stop using the strict, technical, literal implementation of the law to mask an ultimate intent to maintain the status quo and to perpetuate racial segregation and discrimination. This message was fundamentaly important for the civil rights movement. It indicated that some prestigious judges would not fail to see what virtually everyone already knew; namely, that "the civilizing hand of law" could be politely abused if it is in the clutches of people with uncivilized motives and goals. Indeed, as Judge Parker stated decades earlier: courts of equity are neither blind nor impotent.

This recognition, as much as any particular majority decision at any given point, was one of the greatest contributions of some federal judges throughout this long odyssey toward racial justice. This is why Burke Marshall's well-intended, but overly simplistic lecture on federalism missed the mark. This is why many civil rights protesters during those dynamic years (and some of us were there) could fight off mounting frustration and feelings of despair and rejection.

During those turbulent days of the civil rights movement in

the '50s and '60s, the federal courts, and especially the Supreme Court, offered an opportunity for the society to maintain at least a modicum of legitimacy vis-a-vis civil rights protesters. The cases were not always won; the arguments were not always agreed with. But the process for the most part was respected, and some judges at least refused to wink in the face of otherwise devious devices of defiance and difficult definitions of balance of powers and federalism. When civil rights protesters heard some judges articulate the sorts of things Justice Warren (and Judge Johnson)— Cox, Clayton, and others notwithstanding—were articulating, those protesters not only knew they had allies. The fact is that those judges were in a real sense maintaining the integrity of a socio-political system—*a national system*.No more important point could be made.

IV

This paper began with the assertion that the traditional civil rights movement in this country was concerned first and foremost with ending *de jure* segregation. It was a movement for civil *rights*. It was a struggle embedded in legal doctrine and constitutional principles, relying heavily, precisely because it was so legalistic, on moralism to make its case. It hired lawyers, recruited plaintiffs, and went to court, filing class-action lawsuits, taking depositions, arguing motions, distinguishing previous decisions. Civil rights proponents amassed "evidence," and fashioned imaginative constitutional arguments to overcome ingenious efforts at constitutional subterfuge.

On the other hand, the politics of ethnicity (and by extension, American politics generally) has always been a struggle for resources, a struggle to capture and control public office and the ability to dispense patronage and divisible and indivisible benefits. Instead of nurturing and training lawyers and plaintiffs, ethnic politics focused on precinct captains and patronage. Voters properly mobilized, not evidence clearly presented, were the main weapons.

As the civil rights struggle evolved from "rights" to "resources," as it did beginning mainly in the 1960s, it took with it the orientation and the language of the earlier struggle. Thus, it is not coincidental that a "welfare rights" movement developed in the later 1960s. Likewise, an emphasis on certain *legal remedies* to compensate for past discrimination began moving, for instance, in the direction of greater and more specific codification of such policies as "affirmative action." Other groups, notably feminists, started to go to court advocating "comparable worth." And who is unaware of the burgeoning public interest groups in the late 1960s and early 1970s insisting on "rights" of environmentalists, the elderly, the handicapped, students, children, etc. What many Americans had seen as matters over which politicians once had bargained were now becoming public goods and services to which legal claims were laid. Also in the field of voting rights. Now the discussion is not over the *right* to vote, but more over dilution of the vote, what constitutes adequate representation, legality of run-off primaries, and the like.

Some people, once advocates in the earlier civil rights movement, are now disturbed by these subsequent developments toward claiming a legal "right" to resources.[25] They see the earlier struggle for *individual* rights (Apter's secular libertarian model) being turned into a struggle for *group* rights. In this sense, they oppose group-based affirmative action demands. They also question legal efforts in some states to redraw political boundary lines to insure greater possibility for success at the polls, for instance, for blacks. If the one model emphasized individual rights, Apter's second principle of legitimacy was labeled the model of "sacred collectivity." Here, emphasis is on the group, and more concerted, centralized policies are needed to enhance *group* development. The values of the secular-libertarian model are called into question, because of the long-standing discrepancy between theory and practice.[26]

The implications of these developments for our subject—the role of federal law and the courts—are clear, if albeit, problematic.

The Supreme Court in the next several years will not, in all likelihood, be the Warren-like Court inclined toward a liberal, experiential interpretation of the constitution. At the same time, blacks and their progressive allies will be able to exert much more strategic influence in the "political" arena, especially in designated state and local areas and in specific congressional districts. Congress will not be the laggard it once was in the years leading into the 1950s and 1960s.

All these phenomena add new dimensions to the civil rights policymaking process. There will be more institutional actors involved, making the role of the judicial system no less important, but certainly not necessarily, as it once was, in the vanguard. Students of the American governing process ought to find this attractive. Whatever were the strengths and weaknesses, the contributions and distractions of the judicial process to the earlier civil rights movement, it is likely better that that process not be required to shoulder so much of the burden (as it did before) of maintaining a viable body politic. Because the other branches of government were not responsive to often-perceived legitimate demands of the civil rights advocates, the courts had thrust upon them the task of preserving systemic legitimacy. As has been shown, the courts performed this task, on balance, quite well during a crucial period in this country's modern history. But no one democratic institution should have such an awesome responsibility too often. Hopefully, the advocates of "*right* to resources" will be able to utilize the companion branches of government—executive, legislative, *and* state and local—in making their "case."

Commentary / Mark V. Tushnet

These comments offer a series of qualifications to points made in Professor Hamilton's paper. Some of them are a lawyer's comments about the scope of the Constitution, but others are observations about the role of the courts, and especially the Supreme

Court, in the social order. They can be summarized in this way: Professor Hamilton somewhat overstates the role that the courts played in the civil rights movement of the 1950s and 1960s.

Political scientists have convincingly demonstrated that the courts are part of the governing coalition of the nation,[1] and that their output will not often or substantially deviate from the outcomes produced by the other elements in the governing coalition. Occasionally, on some issues, the courts may be slightly ahead of the other branches, but they will also occasionally be behind them. That is how the courts acted with respect to the civil rights movement. If so, that casts some doubt on the proposition, also suggested by Professor Hamilton, that there was some inherent strategic advantage to a "legal" rather than a "political" attack on segregation.[2] For example, if we divided the period from 1940 to 1970 into segments long enough to contain the evolution of dynamic political and legal processes—four to five years—each period would contain varying, but always non-trivial, amounts of all the strategic possibilities, including lobbying in legislatures, litigation in the courts, and direct action in the streets. Nor should that be surprising: The civil rights movement contained many organizations, each of which developed certain specialties in political action, and the courts were only one element in the governing coalition that had to be altered.

Two lines of argument will suggest that the courts were neither much ahead of nor much behind the rest of the governing coalition. First some doctrinal aspects of constitutional law will be examined and the performance of the courts and Congress will be compared. Then a similar comparison will be made based on a slightly different organization of the material, concerned with substantive constitutional law.[3]

Governments can act with respect to oppression in four ways. First, they can exercise their power oppressively, by employing rules that explicitly draw lines on the basis of race,[4] or by intentionally imposing disadvantages on blacks without using rules that draw racial lines. Second, they can exercise their power oppressively by employing rules that do not draw racial lines and administering them fairly, but in a context where the effect is oppressive. Third, government may stand aside and let private power act oppressively if the holders of private power want to do so.[5] Finally, governments can prohibit private oppression.[6]

How did the courts and Congress deal with these four types of oppression? First, consider the courts. As to explicit and intentional discrimination, the Supreme Court up to 1970 outlawed some forms, most dramatically in the desegregation cases and in the Tuskegee apportionment case.[7] But it should be emphasized that the Court here engaged in no doctrinal innovation directly responsive to the civil rights movement's new activities. The prohibition on intentional discrimination had been the stated law since the post-Reconstruction cases of *Strauder v. West Virginia* and *Yick Wo v. Hopkins*.[8] Further, the Court since 1920 had consistently enforced that prohibition.[9]

Second, as to neutral rules the Court did very little. For example, it upheld literacy tests, though it did strike down at least certain forms of the poll tax.[10] Third, it similarly did little about oppressive exercises of private power. With great doctrinal difficulty, it eventually struck down the white primary and restrictive covenants.[11] But between 1950 and 1960 it acted favorably to blacks in only a few rather peculiar cases.[12] Yet there was a pattern, which is of some significance. If the Court did not aggressively protect the interests of blacks, neither did it deal them visible and significant defeats. As will be suggested, that may be the final verdict on the Court's behavior overall.

In the 1950s, then, the courts were doing something to advance the interests of the civil rights movement, but not very much. Congress, though, was doing almost nothing. In the 1960s, the picture changes dramatically. Where the Court was inactive, Congress was vigorous, and where the Court was active, Congress was even more so. As to neutral rules neutrally applied, Congress outlawed state practices that had discriminatory effects on voting, in the Voting Rights Act of 1965. And Congress sim-

ilarly directed its attention to private discrimination in the Civil
Rights Acts of 1964, as to public accommodations and employment, and of 1968, as to housing.[13] These were matters about
which the courts had theretofore had very little to say.

Now the same issues will be examined by regrouping them,
moving away from doctrinal categories and towards more social
ones, including voting rights, rights of civil rights demonstrators,
and education. Then suggestions will be made about how this
argument relates to Professor Hamilton's discussion of problems
of federalism, and the conclusion will suggest the ways in which
the courts *were* important to the civil rights movement.

As Professor Hamilton stresses, from early on the Supreme
Court stated that it would proscribe state voting practices that,
even if neutral on their face, disingenuously were designed to
restrict the voting opportunities of black citizens.[14] Yet it is
important to emphasize as well that the practices to which the
Court directed its attention were quite marginal to the maintenance of the Southern system of race discrimination, at least in
the Deep South. The white primary cases were the most significant, and it is probably significant too that these were the cases
with which the Court had the greatest difficulty.[15] Further, it
seems clear that, again considering the Deep South only, blacks
gained little effective political power as a result of the invalidation
of the white primary.[16] The reason for the limited effect of these
decisions is related to the doctrinal basis for the Court's difficulty
with them. They were hard cases, or so the Court thought,
because they involved practices that were arguably adopted by
purely private actors. Whenever it faced the issue, the Court
found that state decision-makers were sufficiently involved in the
practices to justify the Court's decision to make them comply
with the Constitution. But when no state actors were involved,
the Court thought that it could not impose constitutional requirements. And, until the late 1960s, the Court did not interpret the
statutes, enacted decades before by Reconstruction Congresses,

to authorize the imposition of duties on actors not associated with the state.[17] Yet surely the main reasons for restricted black voting in the Deep South was the private regime under which blacks who attempted to exercise their formal rights to the franchise were intimidated, fired from their jobs, and the like. Eventually the Court did reconstrue the Reconstruction era statutes, overcoming its reluctance to displace state authority in the regulation of private conduct. But by then the civil rights movement had already accomplished a great deal without the courts' direct assistance.

A second example from the voting rights area is the literacy test. Here the Court expressly declined to hold literacy tests unconstitutional, absent a showing that the tests were administered in a discriminatory manner. It would have been quite difficult to make that showing in ordinary litigation on a case-by-case basis. The Voting Rights Act of 1965 adopted innovative techniques that substantially reduced the ability of Southern officials to restrict black voting. Courts did not develop the powerful devices of suspending voter qualification tests in areas that failed to satisfy certain mathematical trigger formulas, or the requirement that changes in voting regulations be cleared with the Justice Department or the courts. As is well known, the great increases in black registration in the South occurred after, and as a result of, the enactment of the Voting Rights Act, not as a result of judicial action.[18]

As has been suggested, even the Voting Rights Act alone might not have been effective in the absence of a strong civil rights movement ready to defend people against private acts of retaliation. That movement too developed largely independent of judicial rupport. Indeed, it is one of the major comments on the Warren Court that it struggled repeatedly to avoid deciding whether the acts of the sit-in protesters of the 1960s were protected by the Constitution.[19] As is now known, the Court came close to rejecting the claims of the demonstrators in *Bell v.*

Maryland.[20] Here too it was Congress that rescued the Court.
The Court seized on one provision of the Civil Rights Act of 1964
and creatively construed it to displace state authority to punish
those who took part in the sit-ins.[21] Yet once again the Court's
contribution to the civil rights movement should not be under-
emphasized. Though it may not have given the movement the
outright victory that the movement sought, neither did the Court
reject the claims made by the protesters. By avoiding the central
questions while repeatedly reversing convictions of protesters,
the Court allowed the movement to continue to believe that
protesters would ultimately be vindicated. Judicial decisions thus
kept alive the possibility of direct action tactics, and in this way
show that the different institutional elements in the governing
coalition can interact in ways that reinforce or even prod other
institutions into action.[22]

Finally, there is education. Here of course *Brown v. Board of
Education* stands as a monument to substantial judicial activity in
support of civil rights. But it is again important to qualify one's
comments. The decision had an immediate effect in border
states, but had essentially no effect in the Deep South until 1970.
Then the Department of Health, Education, and Welfare, armed
with portions of the Civil Rights Acts, began a large-scale program of administrative enforcement of desegregation in the Deep
South. The Court of Appeals for the Fifth Circuit then piggy-
backed on the HEW approach, using the Department's administrative requirements as standards in constitutional cases.[23] The
best interpretation of the courts' performance in the area of
education is this: The Supreme Court had briefly gotten ahead of
the rest of the governing coalition, and when it realized that it
had gotten out of step, it pulled back for about a decade, during
which political changes in other elements of the coalition made it
possible for the courts to resume the activities that they had
earlier cut back on. In light of this history, it seems best to
understand *Brown's* contribution to the civil rights movement as
consisting primarily in the moral support it gave to civil rights

activists, the message they received in 1954 that at last someone in the national governing coalition was fundamentally on their side, rather than in its effects on segregated education per se.

Although these important and complex issues have been dealt with only superficially, that should be enough to indicate that the legal response to the civil rights movement was a collaboration among the branches of government, in which the courts did not play a distinctively supportive role—on some issues, and at some times, they did, but not systematically and across-the-board. Professor Hamilton's comments on federalism during the Kennedy Administration bear this out. For during that time, notions of the appropriate relationship between the federal and state governments were undergoing a substantial transformation within the governing coalition. In response to the political pressure generated by the civil rights movement, Congress was beginning to assert the powers that the Constitution gave it. But a strong tradition in constitutional law suggested that, at least after some point, Congress might go too far in altering the relative responsibilities of the states and the nation. It became clear that notions of federalism had been definitively transformed only when the Supreme Court upheld the constitutionality of the Civil Rights Act of 1964, relying on Congress' power to regulate interstate commerce,[24] and of the Voting Rights Act of 1965, relying on Congress' power to enforce the Reconstruction Amendments.[25] Given the constitutional context in which he was operating, it is not surprising that Burke Marshall took the position that he did, for he was speaking in the middle of that process of conceptual reorientation.[26]

As was indicated at the beginning, the comments do not mean to suggest that the courts were unimportant in the civil rights movement. In conclusion three ways in which the courts mattered can be identified. The first is largely technical. The Supreme Court responded to the civil rights movement at least as much on the level of procedure as on the level of substantive constitutional law. In a series of decisions the Court gave new vigor to a variety of procedural devices that allowed civil rights litigants to challenge state practices in the federal courts. These procedures included the use of three-judge district courts, an institution first established in 1911 and expanded by statutory interpretation in the 1950s,[27] injunctions issued by federal courts against criminal prosecutions in state courts,[28] and an incredibly creative use of the procedure allowing civil rights activists to force state prosecutors into using federal courts as the fora for criminal prosecutions even under state law.[29] These decisions gave activists in the civil rights movement room to breathe and to continue to conduct the protest activities that were, in the end, more important than judicial decisions on the merits of their constitutional claims.

The second way in which the courts mattered does involve the decisions the courts made on the merits. As suggested above, it was important that the courts did not *reject* the substantive claims made by civil rights activists. This failure did more than allow activists to continue to press their innovative legal claims; it also gave them the sense that at least one part of the national government was on their side, albeit giving somewhat less assistance than might have been desired. In this way the courts contributed to the development of political pressure on the other parts of the national government.

Finally, as Professor Hamilton indicates, the courts mattered to the civil rights movement because they gave some legitimacy to the claims of legal right being made by the movement. As has been emphasized, it was not that the courts always endorsed those claims. But their indirect support produced a more general "rights consciousness" that made participants in the movement, and perhaps more important their supporters on the sidelines, more assured of the righteousness of their cause, whether or not the courts ultimately agreed with them. It would go beyond the appropriate limits of a comment on Professor Hamilton's paper to explore the consequences of the development of this "rights consciousness." But it seems important to note that one interpretation on the part of Professor Hamilton's argument is that he believes that "rights consciousness" ultimately over-extended itself, provoking, among other things, a backlash that helped undermine the original claims of right that the civil rights movement of the 1950s and 1960s had made.

The End of One Struggle, The Beginning of Another

WILLIAM H. CHAFE

In 1978 scores of veterans from the Student Non-Violent Coordinating Committee (SNCC) gathered in New York City to honor Ella Baker, the woman who had presided over the recruitment of most of them to the civil rights struggle. The occasion was her 75th birthday. Many of the people in the room had not spoken to each other for years, separated in some cases by distance, in others by political divisions. Now they were reunited to celebrate the wisdom, the humor, and the courage of someone who had transcended all the differences that existed between them.

On that evening, Vincent Harding—one of the spiritual leaders of the movement—spoke to the meaning of the intervening years. Those who claimed that nothing had been achieved by the civil rights movement, he declared, had forgotten what life was like in a Jim Crow America where lynchings went unpunished and terror was everywhere. The movement had achieved a dramatic victory. Yet, Harding went on, the ultimate lesson of the struggle was that all movements for freedom change. As understandings deepen, as issues are redefined, and as the subtleties and effectiveness of one's opposition increases, the struggle for dignity and equality must also evolve, finding new voices, building new alliances, devising new tactics in order to "keep on keeping on."[1]

Vincent Harding's words provide an appropriate context for assessing the impact and results of the civil rights movement. Without question, the movement for black freedom and equality constituted the most important domestic development of post-

127

war America—arguably, the most important domestic event in the 20th century. The civil rights movement provided the energy, the inspiration, and the model for virtually every effort of social reform that emerged in the remarkable decade of the 1960s. The women's movement, the anti-war movement, the student movement, the movement to end poverty, the struggle for Indian rights, Chicano rights, and gay rights—none of these would have been conceivable were it not for the driving force of the civil rights movement. If the movement achieved nothing more than to provide the leadership for other social activists in the 1960s and 70s, this alone would be sufficient.

But the civil rights movement was much more. It toppled segregation, destroyed discrimination within the law against the blacks and members of other minority groups, led to the massive increase in the franchise accomplished by the Voting Rights Act of 1965, paved the way for countless legal and political battles to abolish economic discrimination under the 1964 Civil Rights Act, and achieved—albeit a hundred years late—the legal rights to full citizenship deferred at the end of the First Reconstruction. In addition, during the course of achieving these victories, the civil rights movement laid bare the political, cultural, and structural barriers to complete equality that persist with enormous power to this day, in American society.

It is now known that race is only one of the vehicles for denying people autonomy and freedom. In a different form, but with almost equal devastation, gender and class function in a similar way. From the beginnings of our country, the three forces together—gender, class, and race— have largely shaped a person's life chances. Whether one was born male or female, rich or poor, black or white, determine the power one could exercise, the opportunities available for a career, the emotions it was deemed appropriate to express, the rights one could lay claim to. But for most of this period, attention focused on one or the other of the three. Despite occasional alliances of workers with civil rights advocates, or of feminists with immigrant garment workers and

black sharecroppers, the emphasis of social activists seeking freedom for one group tended to be on their own specific objectives
rather than on the interlocking way in which the different forms
of oppression reinforced each other. Thus women suffragists in
the 19th century disassociated themselves from the 14th and 15th
amendments, and trade union leaders eschewed the recruitment
of women or blacks. The result was that whenever movements for
social change came too close to success, opponents could use the
strategy of divide and conquer to pit against each other those who
were the greatest victims of inequality. Today, we understand the
intersection of gender, class, and race better than we ever have
before, and in large part the reason for this is the way in which
the civil rights movement has helped to highlight that intersection through both its victories and its defeats.

Secondly, the history of the civil rights movement illuminates
the ongoing conflict within American culture between the values
associated with individual freedom and those associated with
collective advancement. If in fact the goal of the freedom movement was to achieve a situation in which each individual could
stand alone to compete as best he or she could, despite the
residual and collective impact of gender, class, and race, then it
must be said that the freedom movement of the 1960s achieved,
at least in the law, the substance of its aims. But if the goal was
rather to assure equality as a result, not just as an idea, then
collective measures are essential—measures that specifically address the ways in which class, gender, and race have functioned in
the past, and function today, to deny freedom and opportunity.
Both in the history of its own goals, and the history of its efforts to
implement those goals, therefore, the civil rights movement
provides a case study of both the limitations and possibilities of
reform in our society.

Perhaps the most important place to start in an effort to understand the civil rights movement is to recognize that its strength
was rooted in the collective solidarity and vitality of black institutions. To this day, many whites tend—mistakenly—to identify the

1960s civil rights movement as a band of integrated marchers
proceeding to the Lincoln Memorial. In fact, the movement to
destroy segregation drew its inspiration from all-black segregated
institutions. The young people who led the sit-in movement in
Greensboro went to Shiloh Baptist Church, an all-black con-
gregation. The minister of that church had taken part in civil
rights demonstrations while a student at Shaw, an all-black college in Raleigh. Many of the protestors had received their introduction to civil rights in the all-black NAACP Youth group in
Greensboro. They were graduates of all-black Dudley High
School, where they had encountered teachers who used the
classroom to exhort them to be the best students they could be,
and who used the homeroom period to have them address voter
registration envelopes. Although there were certainly class differences in the black community in Greensboro and elsewhere,
all black citizens lived in the same area of town, prevented from
moving by housing segregation. When the demonstrations began, they were supported by the entire community—old people,
skilled workers, service workers, the employed, and the unemployed. It was a movement that, whatever its goals, spoke for a
united community.[2]

In Mississippi as well, black institutions provided the home-
base for the drive to end Jim Crow. Occasionally ministers and
school principals opposed the efforts of Robert Moses and others
to recruit participants in the struggle. But when the students
walked out, they walked out of all-black high schools, and when
they met together with SNCC workers, they met in black
churches. While class may have been on some people's minds, it
was not a critical issue for people like Amzie Moore, Hazel
Palmer, Hartman Turnbow, or Fannie Lou Hamer.[3]

Despite that collective base, the goals of the movement
seemed very much within the tradition of individual reform
movements in American history. With an optimism about the
responsiveness of American institutions that seems naive in today's world, the student protestors in Greensboro and the civil

rights workers in Mississippi believed that they could achieve "Freedom Now." If only the laws that sanctioned racial discrimination and the signs which said "white only" were abolished, they believed, black Americans could achieve equal opportunity and secure their place in the sun. The goal, as conservatives like William Bennett and Terry Eastland enjoy telling us today, was to forget about race, to have color blind admissions to jobs and schools, to have black Americans treated as individuals, with the color of their skin forgotten. [4]

But even as the nation focused on the rhetoric that celebrated individual freedom and integration, there were others in the movement who sustained a vision of larger, more collective, more structural change. Nationalism and collective race advancement, of course, had always been part of the dialetic of black reform efforts. But in the early 1960s as well, there was an emphasis upon the economic sources of oppression and the need for more than just freedom as a right. "The current sit-ins and other demonstrations," Ella Baker told the first SNCC Conference, "are concerned with something much bigger than a hamburger or even a giant sized coke." The students, she insisted, were looking for "a group centered leadership, rather than a leader-centered pattern of organization." Similarly, they sought the collective goals of abolishing economic squalor and educational deprivation. When the SNCC workers who heard Baker went to Mississippi and Alabama and Georgia, they quickly discovered that poverty was as much a source of oppression as racism and that the two were intertwined. Teachers were fired from schools if they advocated racial freedom, sharecroppers were evicted from their land, credit was cancelled. More to the point, poor housing, disease, and depression were part of the daily life of civil rights workers who came to understand that the vote—even the law—offered only a partial answer to the quest for freedom, because, in the end, far-reaching structural change in wealth and income and power were central to achieving equality. [5]

The same sub-theme of economic change was articulated by

Bayard Rustin, a close associate of Martin Luther King, Jr., and A. Philip Randolph. Significantly, the goal of the March on Washington in 1963—a march which Rustin coordinated and suggested—was jobs as well as freedom. His own call for a domestic Marshall Plan emphasized the inextricable connection of racial equality and economic equality. While downplaying his own socialist past, Rustin kept in the forefront of the civil right agenda the need to seek systemic change within America.

In some ways, of course, the war on poverty was a consequence of the civil rights movement's emphasis on economic reform. The civil rights movement brought home to many privileged Americans a new awareness of the connection between racial and economic inequality. Largely as a result of the ethical thrust of the civil rights movement, John Kennedy authorized the campaign to abolish poverty, ordering his aides to draft legislation for the program just two days after his June 8, 1963, speech in which, for the first time, he forcefully identified himself with the struggle for civil rights. Lyndon Johnson continued that effort, eloquently telling Congress in 1965:

> Somehow you never forget what poverty and hatred can do when you see its scars on the hopeful face of a young child . . . It never occurred to me in my fondest dreams that I might have the chance to help the sons and daughters of those students and to help people like them all over the country. But now I do have that chance—[and] I mean to use it . . . I want to be the president who educated young children . . . who helped to feed the hungry . . . to help the poor to find their own way.

That year, 43 per cent of all black families were poor, earning under $3,000 per year. Black unemployment was twice that of white unemployment, with black teenage unemployment 100 per cent higher than black adult unemployment. Fewer than 40 per cent of black teenagers finished high school. Now, with Johnson's commitment, it appeared for a moment at least that there would be a possibility of achieving the economic component of the vision for social change articulated by Ella Baker and Bayard Rustin.[6]

But it was not to be. There were, in effect, three approaches to combatting poverty. The most radical involved a conscious effort to redistribute wealth and income through creating new jobs, building new houses, revitalizing cities, creating a new infrastructure of social welfare institutions, and enacting massive tax reform. But such an approach presumed a collective conflict between those who had power and those who did not, implicitly setting one group against another. Such an approach totally violated Lyndon Johnson's commitment to consensus. The second approach was more quantitative in nature, simply using income transfers such as food stamps and health care to provide enough of a margin for poor people so that they could rise above the level of poverty. The third approach, and the one eventually chosen, was more consistent with traditional American values of individualism. By this strategy, individual poor people would be given a chance to overcome the disabilities that surrounded them, and enabled to "earn" a higher standard of living. Here the emphasis was on eliminating, in the Administration's words, "the handicaps that now deny the poor *fair access* to the expanding incomes of a growing economy." In this scenario, an unequal distribution of power and wealth was not the problem. Rather, it was inadequate availability of opportunity.

In the end, the war on poverty included a combination of transfer payments, educational efforts, and psychological incentives. But basically, it involved an effort to change the *attitudes* of the poor, in Sargent Shriver's words, "to move those in poverty from indifference to interest, ignorance to awareness, resignation to ambition, and an attitude of withdrawal to one of participation."

Even with this approach, it is important to acknowledge that the war on poverty did make a difference. Black family income had risen to 60 percent of white family income by the end of 1968, compared to only 54 per cent in 1965. The percentage of black families earning under $3,000 fell from 41 per cent in 1960 to 23 per cent in 1968. Nevertheless, the war on poverty re-

mained a disappointment overall, with blacks who were concen-
trated in the poorest neighborhoods in the nation actually seeing
their condition deterioriate rather than improve. Instead of being
an unconditional war, the anti-poverty effort, historian Mark
Gelfand has observed, represents "a classic incident of the American habit of substituting good intentions for cold hard cash." The
war on poverty fell victim to another war nine thousand miles
away in Southeast Asia. When the anti-poverty program started
officials anticipated the expenditures would exceed $10.4 billion
per year by 1970. In fact, OEO appropriations never exceeded
more than $2 billion per year under Lyndon Johnson.[7]

In the meantime, many SNCC workers who had begun in 1960
and 1961 full of confidence about America's capacity for reform
had begun to alter radically their understanding of the issues,
rejecting the individualist and integrationist approach associated
with the early movement and opting instead for a collectivist
strategy based on racial solidarity. Although Black Power had
many definitions, its origins were embedded in the political and
economic experiences encountered by SNCC workers during the
mid-1960s. Not only did daily contact with malnutrition, disease,
and economic intimidation convince SNCC workers that systemic
change in the economy was essential for racial equality; the same
workers had also become convinced that the only way to achieve
such change was by establishing an independent political base
through which blacks could define their own agenda, shape their
own strategy, and control their own lives.

Repeatedly, white Americans, however liberal, had defaulted
on promises made. It was not just the FBI agents who stood by
taking notes while black demonstrators were beaten, nor a Justice
Department that refused to file suits in most places where black
rights were systematically denied. It was also "friends" who
seemed to insist on the necessity of deferring to those in power
on issues that seemed fundamental to civil rights workers. Thus,
when Hubert Humphrey, Joseph Rauh and others urged the
Mississippi Freedom Democratic Party (MFDP) to accept a hol-

low compromise at the Atlantic City Democratic Convention in 1964 rather than engage in a floor fight that might bring the victory they deserved, SNCC workers balked. As one Mississippi black woman declared, "to compromise would let Jim Crow be . . . ain't no Democratic Party worth that. We've been treated like beasts in Mississippi. They shot us down like animals. We risked our lives coming here. . . . Politics must be corrupt if it don't care none about people down there."[8]

Ultimately, the Black Power movement represented an affirmation that "race" could not be abolished as a reality in America. It was a source of pride and strength, as well as of discrimination, in American society. To many white Americans, Martin Luther King, Jr., held forth the possiblity that 300 years of history could be erased, that through Christian faith, mutual commitment, and idealistic love, Americans could put behind them the legacy of slavery and Jim Crow and walk together to the promised land. King's message had been instrumental in securing support for the legislative objectives of the civil rights movement, helping to forge the national coalition that resulted in enactment of the Civil Rights Act of 1964 and the Voting Rights Act of 1965. But for many SNCC workers, the utopian vision that had attracted white support represented a delusion that promised to subvert their own changing vision of what was necessary. And so, at the moment when the civil rights movement achieved its greatest success, the movement itself was fragmenting, torn deeply by conflict over both its goals and strategy.

The election year of 1968 represented perhaps the last opportunity to put together a program that would address the issues of class as well as race. Beginning in 1965, Martin Luther King, Jr., had become a leading spokesman for the anti-war movement in the United Sates, convinced that events in Vietnam were inextricably tied to racial justice in America. Simultaneously, he articulated a far broader vision of the connection between racial justice and economic democracy. More and more convinced the legislation which barred discrimination meant little without re-

distribution of wealth and power, King directly linked economic
and racial issues. "We must recognize," he told his staff in 1967,
"that we can't solve our problems now until there is a radical
distribution of economic and political power." Class, he said, was
as important as race.

> The black revolution is much more than struggle for the rights
> of Negroes. It is forcing America to face all its inter-related
> flaws—racism, poverty, militarism, and materialism. It is ex-
> posing evils that are rooted deeply in the whole structure of our
> society. It reveals systemic rather than superficial flaws and
> suggests that radical reconstruction of society itself is the real
> issue to be faced.

Instead of reform, King declared, blacks had to move toward
revolution, to an era that would "raise certain basic questions
about the whole society. . . . We are engaged in a class struggle
. . . dealing with the problem of the gulf between the haves and
the haves-nots."

At the same time, Robert F. Kennedy was emphasizing similar
themes. In the years after his brother's death, he had become
more and more engaged—emotionally—in the struggles of the
poor. "Perhaps we cannot prevent this world from being a world
in which children are tortured," Kennedy quoted in his journal
from Camus, "but we can reduce the number of tortured children."

Abroad, he identified himself with workers in Chile, protestors
in South Africa, anti-war demonstrators at home. He had become, Murray Kempton wrote, "our first politician for the pa-
riahs, our great national outsider, our lonely reproach, the natural
standard held out to all rebels." While never embracing black
power, Kennedy did devote more and more attention to the
issues of unemployment, disease, and health in northern ghettos.
"He did things that I wouldn't do," Marion Wright Edelman said,
"he went into the dirtiest, filthiest, poorest black homes . . . and
he would sit with a baby with open sores whose belly was bloated
from malnutrition and he'd sit and touch and hold those babies

. . . I wouldn't do that." Kennedy too talked about the "gulf between the haves and the have nots," expressed his outrage at the institutional violence of poverty and malnutrition, and proclaimed his commitment to dramatic change.

Through parallel paths, both Kennedy and King had come to new understandings of what was necessary in American society to achieve racial justice, and each, in his own way, reached out to forge coalitions that might provide a vehicle for achieving their mutual vision. To many, their efforts represented the last hope for peaceful change using existing political means. With the assassination of both men within two months of each other in the spring of 1968, those hopes crumpled. Perhaps they were doomed from the beginning. Perhaps the notion of transforming America was romantic and utopian. Perhaps those who believed in the goals that Kennedy and King espoused should have found a way to continue.

But instead, those who *opposed* the goals of Kennedy and King—and who in a larger sense opposed the collectivist ideas associated with economic equality and black power—appealed successfully to traditional American values and assumed power. Richard Nixon was now President, the Southern strategy reigned supreme in the White House, and American society and politics took a new direction. In the history of the civil rights movement and the movements it spawned for social and economic equality, 1968 represented a critical turning point away from the possibility of collective solutions to structural inequality.[9]

Instead, supporters of the civil rights movement found the years after 1968 relatively bleak. To be sure, school desegregation advanced more rapidly than at any time since the *Brown* decision, and with the Supreme Court's ruling in *Swan v. Mecklenburg*, formal resistance by school systems to desegregation finally collapsed. There were gains as well in affirmative action, and even the Nixon administration supported the "Philadelphia plan" which mandated a quota of minority employees in construction projects funded by federal dollars. Counter-balancing these policies, however, was a systematic campaign by Republicans—subsequently brought to culmination under Ronald Reagan—to recruit white southerners to their party, using pronouncements against civil rights organizations as a primary recruitment tool. Nixon denounced busing, sought judicial appointments that would please conservative white southerners, and mobilized a political constituency based upon loyalty to traditional values of law and order, often seen as code words for racism. Government programs of infiltration and subversion divided militant black groups, with agent provocateurs providing the occasion for deploying police power to intimidate or destroy militant groups. In one year alone, twenty-eight Black Panthers fell victim to police bullets.[10]

Disorganized and divided, civil rights groups lost a sense of coherence and direction. No one took the place of Dr. King as a national black spokesman, or leader of a potentially united movement. SNCC and CORE fell apart before the divisive politics of Black Power: SCLC floundered without clear direction; and the NAACP and Urban League struggled just to retain their traditional constitutencies. Among other things, the fate of these civil rights organizations reflected their own success. There was no longer a visible, dramatic, clear-cut enemy. It was hard to mobilize a march when there was no theatre to desegregate, no county courthouse to picket over disenfrachisement. The profound problems which remained—institutional racism, unemployment, absence of capital—did not lend themselves to simple slogans or easy solutions. To the extent that a social movement requires transcendent symbols around which to organize, the early 1970s offered few vehicles for collective mobilization. On top of everything else there developed a widespread revulsion against the activism of the 1960s, especially its more militant form, as though someone had administered a massive anti-activism innoculation to the nation. Even Watergate worked to the disadvantage of civil rights groups, focusing the nation's attention on preserving the constitutional processes of government, and thereby helping to divert attention from agendas for further social and economic change.

Significantly, the major movement to retain vitality and direction in the new era of conservatism—feminism—was the last movement to grow out of the civil rights struggle. As it evolved, the women's movement in many ways paralleled the civil rights struggle. The National Organization for Women was started in 1966 in order to secure compliance with the provisions of the 1964 Civil Rights Act which prohibited discrimination on the basis of sex as well as race in employment practices. Like the NAACP, NOW worked within existing political and economic structures to seek reform, using litigation, lobbying, and legislation to counter discrimination against women and to broaden access to equal opportunity. The women's liberation movement, the more radical wing of feminism, grew out of SNCC and SDS. Composed primarily of younger women, supporters of women's liberation had encountered traditional attitudes of male dominance and exploitation within the civil rights struggle. Initially, black women and white women within SNCC cooperated to protest their treatment as second-class citizens, but as black power became more and more a salient force within SNCC, white women began to organize their own movement, both within SDS, and in university communities throughout the nation. Supporters of women's liberation challenged every dimension of the social, economic, and cultural barriers that existed against women. In many ways paralleling SNCC, they frequently endorsed radical economic programs, as well as a strategy of separatism and self-help. On occasion, members of the women's liberation movement attempted to strike alliances with civil rights groups and workers groups, but for the most part, feminism was perceived by both working women and blacks as a primarily white middle class movement. Black women responded more favorably to "feminist" issues like equal pay, child care, and abortion rights than any other group in the population, but most felt that race was the primary issue in their lives, and that joining the struggle to

abolish gender discrimination must take second place to the
central question of abolishing racial discrimination.[11]

In this context, the primary feature of the 1970s and early
1980s has been an almost schizophrenic pattern of progress and
decline for former victims of discrimination, with those who are
above a certain economic level able to take advantage of the
triumphs of the 1960s, while those below a certain economic level
have found the texture of their lives deteriorating to the point of
resignation and defeat. Hundreds of thousands of black Americans were able to take advantage of the gains of the 1960s to
progress swiftly into the mainstream of American economic life.
With the Civil Rights Act of 1964, the Voting Rights Act of 1965,
and the Housing Act of 1968 removing legal obstacles to employment, political participation, and dreams of moving into a house
of one's choice, many blacks were able to claim the benefits of
complete participation in a way of life previously limited to those
with a white skin. Those in a position to do so moved ahead to
maximize the opportunity available, and in the process helped to
transform their lives.

Economic statistics offer one barometer of some of the gains
made possible by the civil rights movement. The number of
blacks living in poverty, for example, declined from over 40 per
cent in 1959 to nearly 20 per cent in 1968. In the meantime the
proportion of black families earning more than $10,000 a year
leaped from 13 per cent in 1960 to 31 per cent in 1971. Although,
overall, black incomes still averaged only 59 or 60 per cent of
white income, that was still an increase over the 48 per cent of
1959. In many areas of the country the gap was still narrower.
Outside of the South, husband and wife two-income families
earned 88 per cent of what white two-income families received.
In 1977, twenty-five to twenty-nine year old black males who
graduated from high school earned 75 per cent of what their
white peers earned, and black men with college degrees earned
93 per cent as much as their white counterparts. Among employed black women, 34 per cent were in the technical, sales, and

administrative support categories by 1980—more than double the percentage of a decade earlier—and only 2 per cent less than the figure for white women. The Voting Rights Act, meanwhile, led to substantial gains in political representation, with black mayors elected in such large cities as Los Angeles, Detroit, Oakland, Atlanta, and Cleveland, and Congressional representation increasing from 4 in 1959 to 18 by 1980.

In the educational arena as well, dramatic changes occurred. The median number of school years for black citizens increased from 10.7 in 1960 to 12.2 in 1970, the latter only .5 per cent less than that for whites. In 1960 only a quarter of a million black Americans were enrolled in the nation's colleges. Seventeen years later, that figure had increased by 500 per cent to 1.1 million, with the U.S. Census Bureau concluding that "among high school graduates, blacks and whites are attending colleges at about the same rate." The average number of visits from corporate recruiters to black colleges soared from 4 in 1960 to 297 in the 1970s, with the increase partly reflected in the rise of black male workers in white collar positions from 16 per cent in 1964 to 24 per cent in 1974 (compared to 40 per cent for whites). In the north, at least, black college graduates could even expect to earn slightly more than whites at entry level positions. [12]

Not surprisingly, some observers described the results as a "story of massive black success." Ben Wattenberg and Richard Scammon concluded that as many as half of all black families had joined the middle class, and even those skeptical of such figures acknowledged that the number of blacks in middle class occupations had increased dramatically. Clearly, the civil rights movement had made a difference.

How then to explain the other side of the coin, the massive decline in life possibilities and economic status for millions of American blacks. In 1954, the unemployment rate among black teenagers was only slightly higher than that for white teenagers. Today it is more than twice as high, and throughout the 1970s, exceeded 40 per cent. Black adult unemployment is twice as high as white adult unemployment, and black teenage unemployment is five times as high as black adult employment. As more and more whites have left America's urban areas, they have been replaced by blacks, but urban dwellers more often than not work in low level service jobs. In 1970, 60 per cent of black men in our central cities occupied such positions in contrast to only 33 per cent of white men. While the percentage of black high school graduates to go onto college is coming closer to that of white high school graduates, the percentage of blacks who *graduate* from high school is falling behind, with only 68 per cent of black males receiving high school diplomas compared to 85 per cent of whites. While some college-educated blacks are enjoying significant success in finding white collar and managerial positions in the suburbs and in corporate America, the number of decent manufacturing jobs and service jobs is declining, leaving thousands of blacks in central cities without employment. New York City experienced a 100 per cent increase in its welfare rolls from 1965 to 1975, and Chicago welfare rolls doubled from 1970 to 1975. By the mid-80s, more than half of all black children under six were living in poverty.

Thus, black America appears to be moving more and more toward a class differentiated social structure. Income differentials among blacks were widening, according to black economist Andrew Brimmer. Indeed, the black sociologist William J. Wilson concluded that divisions among blacks had deepened so much that "now the life chances of individual blacks have more to do with their economic class position than with their day-to-day encounters with whites."[13]

Significantly, a parallel pattern emerged in the status of American women. If college educated and middle-class women proved most receptive to the ideology of feminism, they also appeared to have benefited most significantly from the new ideology. During the 1970s the number of women in college who anticipated entering traditionally "feminine" professions such as elementary and secondary school teaching plummeted from 31 per cent to 10 per cent, while the proportion of women entering law school and medical school mushroomed by 500 per cent. Today most law schools boast entering classes that are at least 40 per cent women. (The figures had been 5 to 8 per cent during the years 1940 to 1960). According to public opinion surveys, growing numbers of college women declared that a career was just as important as marriage in achieving a sense of personal fulfillment, and projections for labor market participation anticipated a job curve for college women that by the year 2000 would parallel that for college men. Although some of the optimism associated with such projections may be suspect, it is undeniable that for some women—especially the college-educated young—changes have occurred in the areas of economic opportunity and personal self-fulfillment that would have been unheard of thirty years ago. It also seems clear that these gains are directly connected to the women's movement and to the civil rights struggle.

But in the case of women as well as of black Americans, the success stories of those who are bright, talented, and from economically secure backgrounds stand in stark contrast to the experience of millions who either live in poverty or whose participation in the labor force consists of dead-end sex-segregated and low paying jobs. Over 80 per cent of all women workers are clustered in just 20 out of the 420 occupations listed by the Census Bureau. Most of these are in the area of service work. Even women who are able to work frequently earn incomes that place them below the poverty level. Approximately 25 per cent of all working women who were head of households with children in 1983 received incomes beneath poverty level.

Experts predict that if present trends continue, by the year 2000 all poor people in America will either be women or children. This startling assessment correlates directly with the massive increase in recent years of female-headed households—a 72 per cent increase during the 1970s alone. A few simple figures tell the impact of that increase. A child born into a family with no father present has one chance in three of being poor; if the family

is headed by a man alone the chances of a child being poor are
one in ten; and if both parents are present the chances of being
poor are only one in nineteen. This "feminization of poverty"
reflects not only structural changes in the job market, with a
decrease in skills and decent paying jobs, but also inadequte
training for better jobs among those caught in the spiral of
downward mobility. More than half of all single-parent families
are headed by people who have never completed high school.
Many of the children who are now poor are the result of teenage
pregnancies, with one out of every six children in the 1970s being
born to a teenage mother. Most frequently these mothers are not
married, have dropped out of school and thus become even more
deeply trapped by poverty. [14]

It is at this point that the intersection of gender, class and race
becomes most clear. While the number of white families headed
by women increased by more than 50 per cent in the 1970s (from
9 to 14 per cent) the number of black families headed by women
now amounts to almost half of all black families. In some inner
city ghettos nearly 70 per cent of all black children are born to
single mothers. As Eleanor Holmes Norton has noted, "you can't
underestimate the stress of raising a child in the ghetto by your-
self, without a grandmother, without an aunt, with no one you
can turn to." In 1978, a female-headed black family earned a
median income of less than $6,000—compared to $16,000 earned
by two-parent black families. Yet one of the reasons black women
were living alone was because there were no jobs for black men.
Unemployment rates for black male teenages of more than 50 per
cent help to explain why black female teenages bear children out
of wedlock and without financial support from the father, particularly in a society where, in many states, welfare payments are
contingent upon there being no male present in the home.

Thus it all becomes a vicious cycle. Young men in the ghetto
cannot find jobs. Young women in the ghetto need welfare to
support their children. Welfare rules discriminate against those
who have a husband present. The end result is that black women

become heads of families descending further into poverty. Welfare becomes a way of life because there is no alternative. In 1980, 40,000 youngsters in New York City dropped out of high school, but of the 105,000 annual job openings in New York, only 9,000 were for messengers, janitors, bus boys, or maids—those occupations available for people without skill or education. The result is an ever-growing group called by some the "underclass," virtually none of whom have completed high school, most of whom are now locked into a cycle of permanent poverty. As a result, even while 35 to 45 per cent of black families have succeeded in achieving a middle class lifestyle, another 30 per cent have experienced a steady decline into ever deeper poverty, totally bereft of gains from the civil rights struggle of the 1960s, captured by the triple burden of gender, class, and race.[15]

Ironically, the gains of desegregation have made even less likely the opportunity to forge a united campaign for improvement based upon racial identity alone. The well-educated, upwardly mobile beneficiaries of changes in the 1960s tend to move out of economically deprived neighborhoods. The home base of church, school, and community organizations that had existed during the era of segregation is gone. And there is an increasing distance between those who are able to take advantage of the opportunities in the mainstream society, and those who are increasingly pressed to the margins of that society, living a life of misery, no longer linked to those better-off than themselves by neighborhood bonds, common institutions, and the shared commitment to racial advancement.

Significantly those who are the chief victims of this new class bifurcation have also suffered a loss of political power. While commentators have widely discussed the decline in voter participation in American elections, the most striking fact of this decline is the class distribution of those who have stopped going to the polls. "When people ask where have all the voters gone," political scientist Walter Dean Burnham has noted, "they should really be asking 'where have all the working class Democrats gone.'" Nearly half of the congressional districts where voter participation declined more than twenty per cent in the 1960s and 70s were in the nation's three largest urban centers—precisely the areas most victimized by poverty, crime, and unemployment. The two congressional districts with the lowest turn out were Bedford Stuyvesant, with an 18.8 per cent participation rate, and the South Bronx, with a 21.8 per cent rate. By contrast, Scarsdale had a turn out rate of more than 70 per cent. The people in these urban areas feel left out, with no stake in government, and no hope that their involvement can make a difference. For such people, the Voting Rights Act of 1965 and the Civil Rights Act of 1964 have little meaning except for the paper that they were written on. What makes this declining voter participation even more devastating is that it has occurred simultaneously with increased mobilization of conservative voters around social issues such as "law and order," "busing," "affirmative action," and welfare.

In the end, therefore, any overall assessment of the civil rights movement must reflect the growing split that has occurred between those able to take advantage of the gains made during the 1960s, and those for whom these gains mean little. Certainly, there can be no gainsaying the extraordinary triumphs recorded in the nation's laws as a result of the civil rights movement, nor the advances made in the aftermath of these laws by large numbers of blacks, women, and others who have individually been able to take advantage of the new opportunities that have developed. If the primary purpose of the civil rights movement is defined as individual freedom, and the opportunity to secure personal gains previously denied on the basis of race, then the movement would have to be described as a complete success. But the civil rights movement had more than the goal of individual freedom. From Ella Baker to Bayard Rustin to Martin Luther King, Jr., its leaders spoke of the collective goals of racial *and* economic equality, narrowing the gap between the haves and the have-nots, creating a situation where all black people, all poor people, all victims of discrimination, would have substantive access to new opportunity as well as simply the theoretical right to advance.

On this second criteria, the verdict must be primarily negative. When the civil rights movement was compatible with the traditional values of individualism and competitiveness in American society, its demands were granted, however reluctantly. But where the movement threatened structural change, questioned deep-seated cultural values, and entered areas that would require a redistribution of political and economic power, resistance set in. Even those "collective gains" that were made, as in the area of affirmative action, now seem in doubt. Not only is the Supreme Court unclear about supporting affirmative action programs; the Reagan administration is adamantly opposed, with enforcement of affirmative action policies down by 75 per cent over the last four years. It would appear that as long as individual reforms do not threaten the basic structure of political and economic power in this society, they can be accepted, regardless of gender or race. But when substantial change of a collective nature is proposed, the going becomes much more difficult.

Unfortunately, while the nation may be arriving at a new understanding of how gender, race, and class intersect to create a two-tiered society, how it attacks this problem is still unclear. If the history of the civil rights movement teaches anything, it is the importance of linking programs for change to values that are widely shared in the dominant culture. Yet all must beware of the fate that occurred during the 1960s, when the collective goals of the movement were separated from the individual goals. In that direction lies a new divide and conquer strategy, with individual success stories used to obscure the massive social problems reflected in the feminization of poverty.

Thus, while acknowledging dramatic gains achieved as a consequence of the civil rights movement, it is necessary, in Vincent Harding's words, to recognize the evolving nature of the struggle, and be open to new alliances, new approaches, new understandings of the collective goals sought. And even though the nature of the movement changes, the fundamental tenet articulated by Frederick Douglass 100 years ago must be remembered: "Power concedes nothing without a demand. It never has and it never will."

Commentary / J. Mills Thornton III

Anyone who hoped that these comments on Professor Chafe's paper would feature something in the way of devasting criticism or stinging rebuttal will be disappointed. While differing with him on one or two of his subordinate points, the commentary will agree with him on the overall structure of his analysis. His trenchant and persuasive argument has, however, prompted some reflections.

The distinction which Professor Chafe draws between the individualist ideal of personal liberty and the collectivist ideal of material equality speaks particularly well to the neglected but highly significant historical problem of why the Civil Rights Movement as a national force ended so suddenly about the time of Martin Luther King's assassination in 1968. The death of the Movement has often been vaguely attributed to the Vietnam War. But that explanation is unsatisfying both temporally and logically. In temporal terms, the war had been going on, albeit at a somewhat lower level, virtually throughout the civil rights years, its escalation had begun in 1964, and by 1968 it had been a full-scale conflict for fully three years. And logic says that if southern blacks' protests against evident discrimination had continued, the sympathy which those protests had aroused would not have been dissipated merely by the fact that those who were sympathetic also had deep commitments in other areas or upon other issues. Indeed, such commitments may well have been mutually reinforcing.

But Professor Chafe's distinction allows one to see the end of the movement in terms which are its own. From the perspective of the ideal of individual liberty, the Civil Rights Movement ended because, with the Civil Rights Act of 1964, the Voting Rights Act of 1965 and finally the Fair Housing Act of 1968, the movement had achieved its goals. In these terms, the movement ended for the same reason that World War II ended: the enemies had been defeated. It is important to emphasize the extent to which this perspective is a valid one. The outpouring of sympathy for the movement on the part of Americans of every sort had been founded upon ideals of individual liberty: equal rights, equal opportunity, equal justice under law, not, as Professor Chafe says, material or physical equality. The very phrase "civil rights" is a term derived from the language of individual liberty; civil rights and civil liberties are assertions about the individual's status vis-a-vis the government and the society; that is, they assert that the citizen has rights as a citizen which the society cannot abridge. It was the evident violation of these principles involved in racial discrimination—the classification of individuals, regardless of their own characteristics, solely on the basis of their race—which had provoked Americans across a broad spectrum to accept the legitimacy of southern blacks' complaints. Nor should we believe that the ideal of individual liberty was not, after all, the one which civil rights leaders themselves held. Professor Chafe is not as clear on this point as he might be. It is true that some elements of the movement's leadership, toward the end, moved on to embrace collectivist ideals. But many important civil rights leaders—including among them Roy Wilkins, Thurgood Marshall and Whitney Young—never did so. And more than that, vast numbers of southern blacks never did so. For blacks in the South, particularly blacks of the middle class, who had known real statutory segregation, segregation by law rather than simply by circumstance, the advances made under the banner of individual liberty were fully apparent; indeed, they were astonishing. Relatively few of them were initially attracted to the doctrines of the young non-Southern blacks who were the leaders of the SNCC radicals. The doctrines of the older civil rights leaders had carried them too far to be deserted readily.

But this observation leads to the other half of Professor Chafe's distinction. He is surely correct that after 1965, a portion of the civil rights leadership began to move away from the ideal of individual liberty towards a collectivist vision. The SNCC radicals certainly fall into this group. For them, the acceptance of collectivism was often explicit, and was at the core of Stokeley Carmichael's slogan, "Black Power." But, as Professor Chafe says, Martin Luther King also clearly moved in this direction in the years from 1965 to 1968. King's collectivism must be distinguished from that of the SNCC radicals, of course. King always rejected Black Power's acceptance of violent revolution, and even more significantly, he rejected its secular materialism. King's own doctrines were at all times founded squarely upon Christianity. But within those bounds, his thought unquestionably turned more and more towards an emphasis on the need for Christian communitarian socialism—what in later years would be called "liberation theology."

These developments did not go unnoticed at the time, though press accounts of them are often presentist and muddled. The triumph of radicalism in SNCC was widely noted. In this regard, a group which was highly significant in shaping national attitudes, though it has been neglected in more recent accounts, was the Deacons for Defense and Justice in Bogalusa, Louisiana. The Deacons were important because they seemed to indicate an acceptance of SNCC radicalism at the grassroots in the black South. And of course, the spread of SNCC radicalism to the Black Panthers in northern California received much attention. But there is a tendency today to forget that King's drift to the left aroused much hostility as well, and in circles which had been previously highly sympathetic to him, such as among prominent Democratic politicians on the national scene.

All of this is by way of saying that the movement of a quite visible portion of the civil rights leadership beyond the standards of individual liberty to the acceptance of collectivist standards in the period from 1965 to 1968 had as much to do with the death of the Civil Rights Movement as did the achievement of its goals, understood in individualist terms. The Civil Rights Movement died, like a fire deprived of oxygen, when it burned beyond American ideals. In doing so, it deprived itself of the broad acceptance and sympathy of Americans which, like oxygen for the fire, had been the element upon which it depended. The collectivist ideals of egalitarian socialism—unlike the ideals of individual freedom and equal rights—were simply not ideals which spoke to the meaning of America as it was generally understood.

In this regard, the one aspect of Professor Chafe's paper that prompts strongest disagreement is his characterization of the attitudes of Robert F. Kennedy. The idea that by 1968 Robert Kennedy had accepted collectivism is, it seems, an absurdity. It is worth noting that as proof of the assertion, Professor Chafe cites only Jack Newfield's sycophantic memoir and Arthur Schlesinger Jr.'s exercise in maudlin romanticism in the guise of history. This is not such evidence as is likely to persuade the dubious. What position papers issued by the Kennedy campaign during 1968 reflect these new collectivist ideals?

However that may be, these general reflections on the death of the Civil Rights Movement lead to a broader point, an effort to place the Civil Rights Movement's demise within the course of American national history taken as a whole. What the new collectivism of the civil rights radicals actually threatened was to force Americans to separate analytically the concepts of freedom and individual rights on the one hand, from the concepts of democracy and equality on the other, and to recognize the fundamental tensions between them. For one hundred fifty years, Americans had spoken of "freedom and democracy," or "liberty and equality" virtually always in a single breath, as if they were mutually reinforcing, interdependent ideas. Now the civil rights radicals called upon Americans, in effect, to see them as antagonistic.

It had not always been so painful to recognize this antagonism, of course. At the founding of the nation, the analytical distinction between the two concepts had been clear. The Founding Fathers had feared democracy and equality precisely because these ideas posed such a threat to liberty. James Madison wrestled with just this problem, for instance, in the tenth Federalist Paper. "The protection," he writes, of "the diversity in the faculties of men, from which the rights of property originate, . . . is the first object of government." But, "From the protection of different and unequal faculties of acquiring property, the possession of different degrees and kinds of property immediately results. . . . Those who hold and those who are without property have ever formed distinct interests in society. . . . The regulation of these various and interfering interests forms the principal task of modern legislation. . . ." How, then, is government to perform its most sacred obligation, the protection of the diversity among people, if by doing so it necessarily creates economic classes in society? Democracy is unequal to the task. He writes, with a barely restrained sneer, "Theoretic politicians who have patronized this species of government, have erroneously supposed that by reducing mankind to a perfect equality in their political rights, they would at the same time be perfectly equalized and assimilated in their possessions, their opinions, and their passions." But nothing could be further from the truth, because as he has already noted, "the possession of different degrees and kinds of property" results from the "different and unequal faculties of acquiring property" which are innate in human beings, and the protection of which is "the first object of government." Of course, one could forcibly equalize the possessions of men, destroying the liberty which is the source of the inequality, but of this idea he says, "It could never be more truly said than of [this] remedy that it was worse than the disease." Wishing to destroy liberty in order to end class divisions, he writes, is like desiring to annihilate air because air produces destructive fires. The solution, he concludes, is a representative republic, which will "refine and enlarge the public views by passing them through the medium of a chosen body of citizens, whose wisdom may best discern the true interest of their country and whose patriotism and love of justice will be least likely to sacrifice it to temporary or partial considerations," a representative assembly staffed by "men who possess the most attractive merit and the most diffusive and established characters." Representation, too, allows the republic to extend over a large area, an area so large that it will include a variety of factions sufficient to cancel each other out, or, when there is a common interest, "it will be more difficult for all who feel it to discover their own strength and to act in unison with each other." Thus, "A rage for paper money, for an abolition of debts, for an equal division of property, or for any other improper or wicked project, will be less apt to pervade the whole body of the Union. . . ."

James Madison not only was aware of the distinction which Professor Chafe has drawn between liberty and equality, but he founded his entire case for republicanism precisely upon the distinction. John Randolph of Roanoke was, as was his wont, even more forthright in his affirmation of the distinction. "I am an aristocrat," he proclaimed. "I love liberty. I hate democracy."

In a sense, however, Madison's plan for controlling class divisions in America through republicanism worked so well that it had the effect of blunting Americans' sensitivity to its analytical foundations. As the generation of the Founding Fathers passed from the scene, political theory in America lost its acuity, and slipped into bland mush. With the dawning of the Age of Jackson, eager orators increasingly coupled equality with liberty, defining them as the twin blessings of a form of government now increasingly called democratic rather than republican. While the machinery which Madison and his generation had designed continued to work, Americans lost the intellectual categories which allowed them to understand how it worked.

But even though Americans had forgotten the contradiction implicit in their acceptance of both liberty and equality as goals, the antagonism of the concepts did not itself go away. It is at the core, for instance, of the failure of the Republicans' plans for the newly freed slaves. Having given the slaves freedom and political rights, the Republican leaders expected that the operation of the American system in which the freedmen were now full participants would of itself deliver them equality. The talents and competitive instincts of the freedmen, now released, would allow them to rise to the positions in society from which slavery had earlier, artificially, barred them. But the reality was that, without an economic base from which to compete in the society, the freedmen eventually lost the political rights—and in substantial measure, even the freedom—which the Republicans had accorded them.

It is perhaps black awareness of this earlier tragic collision between freedom and equality in the Reconstruction era which permitted the civil rights radicals nearly a century later to begin to tease apart the concepts which, for a century and a half, American popular ideology had assumed to be a self-reinforcing unity. But it was an analytical insight which the mass of Americans would not—could not—accept. The civil rights radicals, in effect, asked Americans at large to reject the meaning of America as it had been understood since the War of 1812, to pronounce it fundamentally analytically flawed, and to recover the long-lost analytical framework of the Founding Fathers. And more than that, the civil rights radicals asked that, having understood the terms in which America's Founding Fathers had thought, Americans then reject the conclusions which their Founding Fathers had reached in considering these problems, and embrace precisely the positions the rejection of which had formed the foundation of the republic. The acceptance of the collectivist egalitarian ideal represented the repudiation of the fundamental assumptions underlying our constitutional order.

But most Americans never got that far in their thinking. Most Americans refused the intellectual demands of the civil rights radicals at the point at which they demanded that freedom and equality, democracy and individual rights, be distinguished. Americans found themselves in the position of William Blake as he contemplated the possibility that a compassionate and loving God could have created the fierce and pitiless tiger:

When the stars threw down their spears
And watered heaven with their tears,
Did he smile his work to see?
Did he who made the lamb make thee?

It was the "overwhelming question." Could the liberty and democracy which were at the heart of all that was great and good about America be also the very concepts which were defeating her best efforts to eradicate second-class citizenship from the land? It was impossible for Americans to bring themselves to contemplate such a prospect. They could not, and therefore they did not. They turned, instead, on the civil rights radicals who made the demand.

In Professor Chafe's conclusion, he says, quite correctly, that the Civil Rights Movement teaches "the importance"—even the necessity—"of linking programs for change, to values that are widely shared in the dominant culture." It is exactly for that reason that any effort to effect a collectivist egalitarian program such as that which, by implication, Professor Chafe espouses, is doomed inevitably to failure by the entire weight of American history. To conceive of the opposite is to conceive of the nation without a past.

Notes

Notes to THE ORIGINS AND CAUSES OF THE CIVIL RIGHTS
MOVEMENT
By David Levering Lewis

1. Cf., David Levering Lewis, *When Harlem Was in Vogue* (New York: Knopf, 1981), 205–6.

2. Nancy J. Weiss, *Farewell to the Party of Lincoln: Black Politics in the Age of FDR* (Princeton: Princeton University Press, 1983), 202.

3. Pat Watters and Reese Cleghorn, *Climbing Jacob's Ladder: The Arrival of Negroes in Southern Politics* (New York: Harcourt, Brace and World, 1967), 10.

4. Quoted in Harvard Sitkoff, *A New Deal for Blacks: The Emergence of Civil Rights as a National Issue—The Depression Decade* (New York: Oxford University Press, 1981), 91.

5. Ralph Bunche, "A Critical Analysis of the Tactical Programs of Minority Groups," *Journal of Negro Education*, IV (July 1935), 308–20; Henry Lee Moon, *Balance of Power: The Negro Vote* (Garden City: Doubleday, 1948).

6. Watters and Cleghorn, *Climbing Jacob's Ladder*, 21.

7. August Meier and Elliott M. Rudwick, *From Plantation to Ghetto*, (3rd ed.; New York: Hill and Wang, 1976), 279.

8. Quoted in Watters and Cleghorn, *Climbing Jacob's Ladder*, 12.

9. Quoted in Harvard Sitkoff, *The Struggle for Black Equality, 1954–1980* (New York: Hill and Wang, 1981), 70.

10. George M. Fredrickson, *White Supremacy: A Comparative Study in American and South African History* (New York: Oxford University Press, 1982), esp. chapter 6.

11. Crane Brinton, *Anatomy of a Revolution* (1938; reprint ed., New York: Vintage, 1965); Ted Robert Gurr, *Why Men Rebel* (Princeton: Princeton University Press, 1970). Alexis de Tocqueville, *L'Ancien Regime et la Revolution* (Paris, 1856).

12. Cf., seminal controversial essay by Ralph Ellison, "An American Dilemma: A Review," *Shadow and Act* (New York: Random House, 1964), 303–17.

13. Gunnar Myrdal, *An American Dilemma: The Negro Problem and Modern Democracy* (New York: Harper and Row, 1944), I, lxxi.

14. Stanford M. Lyman, *The Black American in Sociological Thought: A Failure of Perspective* (New York: Putnam, 1972), 113.

15. Albert P. Blaustein and Robert L. Zangrando, eds., *Civil Rights and the American Negro: A Documentary History* (New York: Trident, 1968), 379.

16. *The Social and Economic Status of the Black Population in the United States: An Historical View, 1790–1978* (Washington, D.C.: Government Printing Office, 1979), 379; William H. Harris, *The Harder We Run: Black Workers Since the Civil War* (New York: Oxford University Press, 1982), 127.

17. *The Social and Economic Status*, 61.

18. *Ibid.*, 93.

19. Cf., Lewis, *When Harlem Was in Vogue*, 93, and "Parallels and Divergences: Assimilationist Strategies of Afro-American and Jewish Elites from 1910 to the Early 1930s," *Journal of American History*, 73 (December 1984), 543–64, esp. 548–51.

20. Richard Bardolph, *The Civil Rights Record: Black Americans and the Law, 1849–1970* (New York: Crowell, 1970); Richard Kluger, *Simple Justice: The History of Brown v. Board of Education and Black America's Struggle for Equality* (New York: Knopf, 1975).

21. Kluger, *Simple Justice*, 133–8, 274–84.

22. Martin Kilson, "Black Politics: A New Power," *Dissent*, 18 (August 1971), 333–45, 337.

23. Cf., Kluger, *Simple Justice*, 329; Constance McLaughlin Green, *The Secret City: A History of Race Relations in the Nation's Capital* (Princeton: Princeton University Press, 1967), 209–12; Mamie Garvin Fields with Karen Fields, *Lemon Swamp and Other Places: A Carolina Memoir* (New York: Free Press, 1983), chapters 3 and 4; August Meier and David L. Lewis, "History of the Negro Upper Class in Atlanta, Georgia, 1890–1959," *Journal of Negro Education*, 28 (Spring 1959), 128–39.

24. Kluger, *Simple Justice*, 304.

25. Sitkoff, *A New Deal for Blacks*, 251; B. Joyce Ross, *J. E. Spingarn and the Rise of the NAACP, 1911–1939* (New York: Atheneum, 1972), 182.

26. Herbert Hill, "The Racial Practices of Organized Labor: The Contemporary Record," in Julius Jacobson, ed., *The Negro and the American Labor Movement* (Garden City: Anchor, 1968), chapter 8, esp. 287.

27. Ray Marshall, "The Negro in Southern Unions," in Jacobson, ed., *The Negro and the American Labor Movement*, 138; Sitkoff, *A New Deal for Blacks*, 179.

28. August Meier and Elliott M. Rudwick, *Black Detroit and the Rise of the UAW* (New York: Oxford University Press, 1979), 100.

29. Nancy J. Weiss, *The National Urban League, 1910–1940* (New York: Oxford University Press, 1974), 291.

30. William H. Harris, *Keeping the Faith: A Philip Randolph, Milton P. Webster, and the Brotherhood of Sleeping Car Porters, 1925–37* (Urbana: University of Illinois Press, 1977), chapter 7.

31. Sitkoff, *A New Deal for Blacks*, chapter 6; Mark Naison, *Communists in Harlem During the Depression* (Urbana: University of Illinois Press, 1983); Nell Painter, *The Narrative of Hosea Hudson: His Life as a Negro Communist in the South* (Cambridge: Harvard University Press, 1979); Donald H. Grubbs, *Cry from the Cotton: The STFU and the New Deal* (Chapel Hill: University of North Carolina Press, 1971).

32. Watters and Cleghorn, *Climbing Jacob's Ladder*, 27.

33. *Ibid.*, 30.

34. Marshall Frady, *Wallace* (New York: World, 1968), 102.

35. Aldon Morris, *The Origins of the Civil Rights Movement: Black Communities Organizing for Change* (New York: Free Press, 1984); Morton Sosna, *In Search of the Silent South: Southern Liberals and the Race Issue* (New York: Columbia University Press, 1977); Harry Ashmore, *Hearts and Minds: The Anatomy of Racism from Roosevelt to Reagan* (New York: McGraw-Hill, 1982).

36. Kluger, *Simple Justice*, chapter 25; Steven F. Lawson, *Black Ballots: Voting Rights in the South, 1944–1969* (New York: Columbia University Press, 1976), chapter 6.

37. Anthony Lewis, *Portrait of a Decade: The Second American Revolution* (New York: Random House, 1964), chapter 4.

38. Quoted in *ibid.*, 29.

39. Maurine Christopher, *America's Black Congressmen* (New York: Crowell, 1971), 200.

40. Watters and Cleghorn, *Climbing Jacob's Ladder*, 28.

41. Lewis, *Portrait of a Decade*, 40.

42. David Levering Lewis, *King: A Biography* (Urbana: University of Illinois Press, 1978), 93.

Notes to CIVIL RIGHTS REFORM AND THE BLACK FREEDOM STRUGGLE
by Clayborne Carson

1. John Orbell, "Protest Participation among Southern Negro College Students," *American Political Science Review*, 61 (June 1967), 554–555. Cf. Ruth Searles and J. Allen Williams, Jr., "Negro College Students' Participation in Sitins," *Social Forces*, 40 (March 1962), 215–220; James A. Geschwender, "Social Structure and the Negro Revolt: An Examination of Some Hypotheses," *Social Forces* 43, (December 1964), 250–256; and Anthony M. Orum and Amy M. Orum, "Class and Status Bases of Negro Student Protest," *Social Science Quarterly*, 49 (December 1968), 521–533. This literature is more fully discussed in my paper, "The Civil Rights Movement and the Transformation of American Racial Thought," delivered at annual meeting of the Organization of American Historians, Los Angeles, April 5, 1984.

2. Arthur M. Schlesinger, Jr., *A Thousand Days: John F. Kennedy in the White House* (Boston: Houghton Mifflin, 1965), 850, 892.

3. Carl F. Brauer, *John F. Kennedy and the Second Reconstruction* (New York: Columbia University Press, 1977), 318.

4. Havard Sitkoff's survey of the black struggle reflects the common journalistic emphasis on King and the local movements he initiated but nonetheless notes the ideological diversity that accompanied the increasing scale of activism during and after 1963: "The unemployed and working poor had little interest in . . . symbolic and status gains. . . . They had even less sympathy for, or knowledge of, the spirit of *Satyagraha*. King's talk of love left them cold. . . . As the black struggle became more massive and encompassing, impatience multiplied, disobedience became barely civil, and nonviolence often a mere stratagem." Sitkoff, *The Struggle for Black Equality, 1954–1980* (New York: Hill and Wang, 1981), 145.

5. William H. Chafe, *Civilities and Civil Rights: Greensboro, North Carolina, and the Black Struggle for Freedom* (New York: Oxford University Press, 1980); and Robert J. Norrell, *Reaping the Whirlwind: The Civil Rights Movement in Tuskegee* (New York: Knopf, 1985). Norrell comments: "[The civil rights movement] had a different experience in each place and no place was the same after it left. Each community now has a story to tell about the movement, and only when many of those stories are told will the South's great social upheaval be well understood" [p. ix].

6. Cf. J. Mills Thornton III, "Challenge and Response in the Montgomery Bus Boycott," *The Alabama Review*, 33 (July 1980), 163–235; and Aldon D. Morris, *The Origins of the Civil Rights Movement: Black Communities Organizing for Change* (New York: The Free Press, 1984).

7. Cf. August Meier and Elliot Rudwick, CORE: *A Study in the Civil Rights Movement, 1942–1968* (New York: Oxford University Press, 1973), chapter 4; and Carson, *In Struggle: SNCC and the Black Awakening of the 1960s* (Cambridge: Harvard University Press, 1981), chapters 1 and 2.

8. Cf. Meier and Rudwick, CORE, chapter 5; and Carson, *In Struggle*, chapter 6.

9. Schlesinger, *Thousand Days*, 854–855.

10. George Breitman, ed., *Malcolm X Speaks: Selected Speeches and Statements* (New York: Merit Publishers, 1965), 13.

11. Doug McAdam, *Political Process and the Development of Black Insurgency, 1930–1970* (Chicago: University of Chicago Press, 1982).

12. Morris, *Origins of the Civil Rights Movement*, 284.

Notes to CREATIVE TENSIONS IN THE LEADERSHIP OF THE CIVIL RIGHTS MOVEMENT
by Nancy J. Weiss

1. Clayborne Carson, *In Struggle: SNCC and the Black Awakening of the 1960s* (Cambridge: Harvard University Press, 1981), 63, 137, 159; James Farmer, *Lay Bare the Heart: An Autobiography of the Civil Rights Movement* (New York: Arbor House, 1985), 13–14, 186, 189–91, 203–204, 212, 215–18; James Forman, *The Making of Black Revolutionaries* (New York: Macmillan, 1972), 220, 255–56, 314–15, 361–71, 377–78; David L. Lewis, *King: A Critical Biography* (1970; paperback ed., Baltimore: Penguin, 1971), 116–19, 163, 170; Debbie Louis, *And We Are Not Saved: A History of the Movement as People* (Garden City: Doubleday, 1970), 208–18; August Meier and Elliott Rudwick, CORE: *A Study in the Civil Rights Movement, 1942–1968* (New York: Oxford University Press, 1973), 105, 110, 116–17, 119–20, 138, 144, 163–64, 190, 229–31; Aldon D. Morris, *The Origins of the Civil Rights Movement: Black Communities Organizing for Change* (New York: Free Press, 1984), 121–25, 138, 213–14, 242–46, 248–49; Stephen B. Oates, *Let the Trumpet Sound: The Life of Martin Luther King, Jr.* (New York: Harper and Row, 1982), 119, 127–28, 157–58, 197, 199, 251–53, 308, 352–53; Howell Raines, *My Soul Is Rested: Movement Days in the Deep South Remembered* (1977; paperback ed., New York: Penguin, 1983), 213–14; Harvard Sitkoff, *The Struggle for Black Equality, 1954–1980* (New York: Hill and Wang, 1981), 147–48; Robert Penn Warren, *Who Speaks for the Negro?* (New York: Random House, 1965), 145, 155–56; Roy Wilkins with Tom Mathews, *Standing Fast: The Autobiography of Roy Wilkins* (New York: Viking, 1982), 269–70, 285, 319.

2. Morris, *The Origins of the Civil Rights Movement*, 17–25, 40–76, 194, 284. The quotations are from pp. 284 and 194 respectively.

3. Interviews with Jane Lee J. Eddy, Nov. 30, 1983, New York City; Dorothy Height, Dec. 4, 1979, New York City; James Farmer, Aug. 17, 1983, Fredericksburg, Va.

4. Eddy interview (source of the quotation); Height interview; Stephen R. Currier to Martin Luther King, Jr., June 12, 1963, Martin Luther King, Jr.,

Papers, I:1, 8:3, Library and Archives, Martin Luther King, Jr., Center for Nonviolent Social Change; *Newsday*, July 17, 1963, clipping in Whitney M. Young, Jr., Papers, Box 220, Rare Book and Manuscript Library, Columbia University; Stephen R. Currier to Henry Steeger, July 25, 1963, *ibid.*, Box 38; Reese Cleghorn, "The Angels Are White: Who Pays the Bills for Civil Rights?" *New Republic*, CXLIX (Aug. 17, 1963), 12.

    5. Council for United Civil Rights Leadership, Report #1, July 16, 1963, Young Papers, Box 38.

    6. Wilkins quoted in *Newsday*, July 17, 1963; Young quoted in Danville, Va., *Register*, July 9, 1963, clippings in Young Papers, Box 220. See also unidentified CUCRL spokesman, quoted in New York *Herald Tribune*, *ibid.*, Box 7.

    7. Draft of letter from Stephen R. Currier and Whitney M. Young, Jr., Sept. 11, 1963; Council for United Civil Rights Leadership, Report #1, July 16, 1963, Young Papers, Box 38; Currier to Martin Luther King, Jr., July 12, Aug. 8, 1963, King Papers, I:1, 8:3; Farmer interview; Cleghorn, "The Angels Are White," 13; *New York Times*, July 18, 1963. The formula for the distribution of funds, which gave each organization roughly ten percent of its budget for the previous year, left SNCC with by far the smallest allocation, a decision that rankled with SNCC leaders. See Forman, *The Making of Black Revolutionaries*, 366.

    8. On the meetings, see, e.g., Jane Lee J. Eddy memorandum to James Farmer et al, July 11, 1963, King Papers, I:1, 7:28; Stephen R. Currier to Martin Luther King, Jr., July 31, 1963, *ibid.*, I:1, 8:3; Wiley A. Branton memoranda to Members of CUCRL, Oct. 7, 1963, *ibid.*, I:1, 7:28; Nov. 18, 1963, Jan. 17, Feb. 6, June 2, 10, 1964, *ibid.*, I:1, 7:29; Aug. 6, Oct. 14, 1964, Feb. 17, Apr. 12, 1965, *ibid.*, I:1, 7:30; Jack Greenberg to Dear Friend, July 19, 1965, *ibid.*, I:1, 7:30. On the agendas, see, e.g., CUCRL Agenda, Mar. 5, Apr. 27, June 8, Nov. 4, 1964, Young Papers, Box 38; Aug. 11, 1964, King Papers, I:1, 7:30; May 20, 1965, Young Papers, Box 38; Mar. 23, 1966, *ibid.*, Box 54; CUCRL Minutes, May 20, June 17, 1965, *ibid.*, Box 38. On public policy statements, see, e.g., Joint Statement of the Council for United Civil Rights Leadership, July 3, 1964, and Farmer, Forman, Greenberg, Height, King, Wilkins, Young to the President, Nov. 11, 1964, *ibid.*

    9. Farmer interview; Height interview.

    10. Eddy interview; CUCRL Agenda, Aug. 11, 1964, King Papers, I:1, 7:30; CUCRL Minutes, May 20, 1965, Young Papers, Box 38; CUCRL Agenda, Mar. 23, 1966, *ibid.*, Box 54; Farmer interview. Forman, *The Making of Black Revolutionaries*, 365–70, presents an extreme view of the persistence of tensions within CUCRL.

    11. Interview with John Lewis, Aug. 3, 1983, Atlanta.

    12. Height interview; interview with Andrew Young, Aug. 4, 1983, Atlanta.

    13. On funding, see the range of documents in King Papers, I:1, 7:29 and 7:30. On the difficulty of mustering attendance at meetings, see Whitney M. Young, Jr. to Martin Luther King, Jr., Jan. 19, 1966, *ibid.*, I:1, 18:6; Young to James Farmer, Jan. 19, 1966; Jack Greenberg to Young, Jan. 21, 1966; Roy Wilkins to Young, Jan. 28, 1966; Young to King, Feb. 24, 1966, Young Papers, Box 54. On the liquidation of the organization, see Arthur Q. Funn to King, Jan. 30, 1967, *ibid.*, Box 66.

    14. For the elaboration of these models, see, e.g., Alvin W. Gouldner, ed., *Studies in Leadership: Leadership and Democratic Action* (New York: Harper, 1950), 53–66; John P. Roche and Stephen Sachs, "The Bureaucrat and the Enthusiast: An Exploration of the Leadership of Social Movements," *Western Political Quarterly*, VIII (July 1955), 248–61; Joseph R. Gusfield, "Functional Areas of

Leadership in Social Movements," *Sociological Quarterly*, VII (Spring 1966), 137–56 (quotations are from 137 and 142).

15. Gusfield, "Functional Areas of Leadership in Social Movements," 137–42. The quotations are from p. 142.

16. Martin Luther King, Jr., *Why We Can't Wait* (1963; paperback ed. New York: New American Library, 1964), 42; Whitney M. Young, Jr., "Race Relations Leadership—1963," speech to Capital Press Club, Washington, D.C., Feb. 21, 1963, Young Papers, Box 126.

17. Young, "Race Relations Leadership—1963."

18. Carson, *In Struggle*, 2–3 and passim; Cleveland Sellers, *The River of No Return: The Autobiography of a Black Militant and the Life and Death of* SNCC (New York: Morrow, 1973), 117; Elliott Rudwick and August Meier, "Integration vs. Separatism: The NAACP and CORE Face Challenge from Within," in Meier and Rudwick, *Along the Color Line: Explorations in the Black Experience* (Urbana: University of Illinois Press, 1976), 238–60; David Garrow, *Protest at Selma: Martin Luther King, Jr., and the Voting Rights Act of 1965* (New Haven: Yale University Press, 1978), 220–32; Warren, *Who Speaks for the Negro?*, ch. 3; Emilie Schmeidler, "Shaping Ideas and Actions: CORE, SCLC, and SNCC in the Struggle for Equality, 1960–1966" (Ph.D. dissertation, University of Michigan, 1980); Guichard Parris and Lester Brooks, *Blacks in the City: A History of the National Urban League* (Boston: Little, Brown, 1971); Nancy J. Weiss, "Whitney M. Young, Jr.: Committing the Power Structure to the Cause of Civil Rights," in John Hope Franklin and August Meier, eds., *Black Leaders of the Twentieth Century* (Urbana: University of Illinois Press, 1982), 331–58.

19. Martin Luther King, Jr., *Stride toward Freedom: The Montgomery Story* (1958; paperback ed., New York: Harper and Row, 1964), 131–40; King, *Why We Can't Wait*, 107–109; Oates, *Let the Trumphet Sound*, 215, 219, 230–31; Richard Bardolph, ed., *The Civil Rights Record: Black Americans and the Law, 1849–1970* (New York: Crowell, 1970), 522–26.

20. Meier and Rudwick, *CORE*, 138–43; Farmer, *Lay Bare the Heart*, 202–204, 210–12; Anthony Lewis, *Portrait of a Decade: The Second American Revolution* (1964; paperback ed., New York: Bantam, 1965), 247.

21. Garrow, *Protest at Selma*, 141–50; Carl M. Brauer, *John F. Kennedy and the Second Reconstruction* (New York: Columbia University Press, 1977), 239, 246–49, 260–62; Doris Kearns, *Lyndon Johnson and the American Dream* (New York: Harper and Row, 1976), 192.

22. Bardolph, ed., *The Civil Rights Record*, 409; Jo Freeman, "Resource Mobilization and Strategy: A Model for Analyzing Social Movement Organization Actions," in Mayer N. Zald and John D. McCarthy, eds., *The Dynamics of Social Movements: Resource Mobilization, Social Control, and Tactics* (Cambridge: Winthrop, 1979), 175.

23. James Q. Wilson, "The Strategy of Protest: Problems of Negro Civic Action," *Journal of Conflict Resolution*, V (Sept. 1961), 298; Farmer quoted in Warren, *Who Speaks for the Negro?*, 198. Wilson offers an apt illustration of the point: "In New York City, for example, the Urban League often finds itself presented with opportunities for negotiation because an extremist leader, such as Rep. Adam Clayton Powell, Jr., has brought some city agency or private party under heavy fire. This is true even though many Urban League leaders often deplore Powell and his tactics; for them, Powell is a useful nuisance." August Meier makes a similar point about Martin Luther King: "Without CORE and, especially, SNCC,

King would appear 'radical' and 'irresponsible' rather than 'moderate' and 'respectable.'" Meier, "On the Role of Martin Luther King," *New Politics*, IV (Winter 1965), reprinted in John H. Bracey, Jr., August Meier, and Elliott Rudwick, eds., *Conflict and Competition: Studies in the Recent Black Protest Movement* (Belmont, Calif.: Wadsworth, 1971), 88.

24. Jack L. Walker, "The Functions of Disunity: Negro Leadership in a Southern City," *Journal of Negro Education*, XXXII (Summer 1963), reprinted in Bracey, Meier, and Rudwick, eds., *Conflict and Competition*, 55–58. The quotations are from p. 57.

25. *Ibid.*, 60. Walker points to similar examples of "unanticipated cooperation and sharing of functions between protest and conservative Negro leaders" in Knoxville and Winston-Salem. See p. 61.

26. Height interview.

27. Interview with John H. Johnson, Oct. 29, 1984, Chicago.

28. Farmer, *Lay Bare the Heart*, 216.

29. Whitney M. Young, Jr., "The Practice of Racial Democracy," *Conference Board Record*, June 1965, reprint in Young Papers, Box 132; interview with James R. Shepley, Oct. 10, 1979, New York City.

30. Wilson posits two requisites for protest action: "an agreed-upon goal on behalf of which mass action can be mobilized," and "an identifiable group or agency or firm which is capable of granting the end sought" (i.e., "a specific target"). "The Strategy of Protest," 293–94. See also p. 296.

Notes to THE POLITICS OF THE MISSISSIPPI MOVEMENT, 1954–1964
by John Dittmer

I wish to thank professors Neil McMillen, Edwin King, James T. Patterson, and James W. Silver for their thorough criticism of the manuscript.

1. Typed transcript of Mayor Allan Thompson's television address, John R. Salter papers, State Historical Society of Wisconsin, Madison.

2. Typed transcript of Medgar Evers's television address, Salter papers. See also John R. Salter, Jr., *Jackson, Mississippi: An American Chronicle of Struggle and Schism* (New York: Exposition Press, 1979), 119–121.

3. Arnold Rose, *The Negro in America: The Condensed Version of Gunnar Myrdal's "An American Dilemma"* (1948; New York: Harper and Row, 1964), 29.

4. "Report on Mississippi for Board and Staff Reference," 1954, Papers of the National Association for the Advancement of Colored People, Library of Congress.

5. For the definitive history of the Citizens' Council, see Neil R. McMillen, *The Citizens' Council: A History of Organized Resistance to the Second Reconstruction* (Urbana: University of Illinois Press, 1971).

6. During the early summer of 1954 the NAACP requested meetings with local school boards to "seek to formulate plans to abolish segregation." Not surprisingly, no such meetings took place. Jackson *Daily News*, May 29, 1954.

7. David Halberstam, "A County Divided Against Itself," *Reporter* (December 15, 1955), 30–32; memorandum from Ruby Hurley to Roy Wilkins, October 7, 1955, NAACP papers.

8. Mrs. Medgar Evers with William Peters, *For Us, The Living* (1967; New York: Ace paperback edition, 1970), 125, 147, 165–67.

9. United States Commission on Civil Rights, *With Liberty and Justice for All* (Washington: Government Printing Office, 1959), 50–51.

10. *Ibid.*, 50–53.

11. Several months before the attempt on Courts's life, the NAACP had learned that he was "next on the list to go." "Memorandum from Mrs. Hurley," May 13, 1955, NAACP papers. See also New York *Post*, November 30, 1955, clipping in NAACP papers.

12. *Delta Democrat Times*, August 16, 1955; NAACP press release, August 18, 1955; "Are You Curious About Mississippi?" undated press release, NAACP papers.

13. Quoted in David Halberstam, "Tallahatchie County Acquits a Peckerhead," *Reporter* (April 19, 1956), 28.

14. "Statistical Report of . . . Medgar Evers. For Year 1959, January 1–December 5," in NAACP papers.

15. "Memorandum to Mr. White from Mrs. Hurley," October 8, 1952; Ruby Hurley to Roy Wilkins, April 8, 1955; "Information re Killing in Mississippi, Telephoned in by Ruby Hurley, May 13, 1955," NAACP papers.

16. Mrs. Medgar Evers, *For Us, The Living*, 216.

17. Medgar Evers to Ruby Hurley, January 24, 1957, NAACP papers.

18. Amzie Moore was the key figure in the move to bring in activists from outside the state. In the 1950s Moore had close associations with such organizations as the Southern Conference Education Fund (SCEF), and he encouraged Bob Moses to bring SNCC organizers into the Mississippi Delta in 1960 and 1961.

19. Interview with Robert Moses, August 15, 1983.

20. For the sake of brevity, unless otherwise noted the term "COFO" will describe the activities of the more militant SNCC-CORE faction of the Mississippi movement during the early sixties.

21. Leslie Dunbar, interview in the Oral History Collection of the Civil Rights Documentation Project, Howard University, 1968, p. 20.

22. Robert F. Kennedy, recorded interview by Anthony Lewis, in the John F. Kennedy Oral History Program, December 4, 1964, p. 573, John F. Kennedy Library. Robert Kennedy stated that Eastland's advice was "very, very helpful" during the time he was attorney general, and added that "I found it much more pleasant to deal with him than many of the so-called liberals in the House Judiciary Committee or in other parts of Congress or the Senate." *Ibid.*, 527.

23. Burke Marshall interview in the JFK Oral History Program, 1970, p. 41, Kennedy Library.

24. Martin Luther King, quoted in Arthur Schlesinger, Jr., *Robert Kennedy and His Times* (Boston: Houghton Mifflin, 1978), 340. King was referring here to the Kennedys' method of operation in the crisis surrounding James Meredith's integration at the University of Mississippi.

25. Interview with Burke Marshall, December 3, 1983, New Haven, Connecticut.

26. Burke Marshall, interview with Victor Navasky, November 18, 1967, Victor Navasky papers, Kennedy Library.

27. Memorandum from Burke Marshall to Byron White, July 14, 1961, Burke Marshall Papers, Kennedy Library.

28. "Report of the Attorney General to the President on the Department of Justice's Activities in the Field of Civil Rights, Dec. 29, 1961," Presidential Office Files, Kennedy Library. When asked recently to comment on the government's reluctance to initiate similar action in cases after the Hardy episode, former

Justice Department attorney John Doar would state only that the primary role of Justice Department lawyers in Mississippi was to prepare voter registration suits. interview with John Doar, June 14, 1985, New York City.

29. Neil R. McMillen, "Black Enfranchisement in Mississippi: Federal Enforcement and Black Protest in the 1960s," *Journal of Southern History*, XLIII (August, 1977), 356.

30. Pat Watters and Reece Cleghorn, *Climbing Jacob's Ladder: The Arrival of Negroes in Southern Politics* (New York: Harcourt, Brace and World, 1967), 61–62.

31. *Ibid.*, 62; undated note from Frank Smith to the author, November, 1985.

32. For a fascinating account of the Jackson movement of 1962–63 by its chief strategist and organizer, see Salter, *Jackson, Mississippi*.

33. Howard Zinn, SNCC: *The New Abolitonists* (Boston: Beacon, 1965), 99–101; Clayborne Carson, *In Struggle: SNCC and the Black Awakening of the 1960s* (Cambridge: Harvard University Press, 1981), 97–98.

34. Interview with Wazir Peacock, December 13, 1984, Jackson, Mississippi.

35. Interview with Robert Moses.

36. Quoted in Howell Raines, *My Soul Is Rested* (1977; paperback ed., New York: Penguin, 1983), 274.

37. Gloster Current to Roy Wilkins, November 5, 1964, NAACP papers.

38. Gloster Current to Charles Evers, July 17, 1964, NAACP papers.

39. Lee White, "MEMORANDUM FOR THE PRESIDENT," June 17, 1964; White to Aaron Henry, June 18, 1964, Lyndon B. Johnson Library. On June 21, 1964, 268 volunteers sent a plea to President Johnson to "hear your voice in support of those principles to which Americans have dedicated and sacrificed themselves since our country's founding." Nearly two months later the White House sent its reply in a form letter, stating that the federal government was doing all it could in Mississippi, and had sent troops to search for the three missing civil rights workers. Among the signers of the June 21 letter was volunteer Andrew Goodman. Stephen Bingham to President Lyndon Johnson, June 21, 1964; Lee White to Bingham, August 10, 1964, Johnson Library.

40. Interview with Burke Marshall.

41. Robert F. Kennedy, "Memorandum for the President," June 5, 1964, Johnson Library.

42. Pat Watters, *Down to Now: Reflections on the Southern Civil Rights Movement* (New York: Pantheon, 1971), 301.

43. Bob Moses, "EMERGENCY MEMORANDUM," July 19, 1964, copy in Jan Hillegas Collection, Jackson, Mississippi.

44. Carson, *In Struggle*, 125.

45. *Ibid.*, 126.

46. Joseph Rauh, interviewed by Anne Romaine, June, 1966, p. 30; Mendy Samstein, interviewed by Anne Romaine, September, 1965, copies in the Anne Romaine papers, State Historical Society of Wisconsin. See also Anne Cooke Romaine, "The Mississippi Freedom Democratic Party Through August, 1964" (M.A. thesis, University of Virginia, 1970).

47. Ed King, interviewed by Anne Romaine, August, 1965, p. 9, Romaine papers. King was also at the meeting with Humphrey. Ed King's unpublished manuscript on the freedom movement in Mississippi is an extremely valuable insider's view.

48. U.S. Congress, Select Committee to Study Governmental Operations with

Respect to Intelligence Activities, *Intelligence Activities and the Rights of Americans, Book II, Final Report,* 94th Cong., 2d Session, April 26, 1976, pp. 117–18.

49. President's Diary and Diary Backup, August 15–26, 1964, Johnson Library.

50. Interview with Robert Moses.

51. Ed King, interviewed by Anne Romaine, 8–9.

52. Interview with Robert Moses.

53. *Ibid.;* Ed King, interviewed by Anne Romaine, 8.

54. Interview with Robert Moses.

55. Unita Blackwell, interview in the Oral History Collection, Howard (1968), 17.

56. Charles Sherrod, undated and untitled manuscript, Charles Sherrod papers, State Historical Society of Wisconsin. See also Sherrod, "Mississippi at Atlantic City," *Grain of Salt* (Union Theological Seminary), Oct. 12, 1964.

57. Interview with David Dennis, July 12, 1983, Lafayette, Louisiana.

58. Bob Moses, "Remarks at SNCC's First Western Conference," in *Pacific Scene* (Feb., 1963), 2–5.

59. "Memorandum from Curtis B. Gans to Leon Shull," November 20, 1964, in Americans for Democratic Action Papers. Steven Gillin, who is preparing a book on the ADA, provided me with a copy of this memorandum.

60. Quoted in Jack Newfield, "The Liberals' Big Stick," *Cavalier,* June, 1985, p. 34.

61. Interview with James Forman, May 7, 1985, Washington, D.C. Bob Moses recalls that "there was no way to take that disagreement [over FDP strategy] to the people without clashing with Guyot at that point." Interview with Robert Moses.

62. Middle-class blacks with formal education were also embarrassed at the rise of a group of leaders who lacked much schooling. Bob Moses has stated that both state and national civil rights leaders believed that black "leadership should somehow be filtered through an education process." Interview with Robert Moses.

63. Ed King, interviewed by Anne Romaine, 10.

64. See Gloster Current to Bishop Stephen G. Spottswood, and Members of the Board, "Re: NAACP Withdrawal from COFO," December 29, 1964, NAACP papers.

65. For insight into the bitterness which had developed between COFO activists and NAACP stalwarts, see "Minutes of the COFO Convention," March 7, 1965, copy in The Archives of Labor History and Urban Affairs, Wayne State University.

66. The Freedom Democratic Party's problems with Washington increased when in the summer of 1965 the FDP *Newsletter* reprinted a leaflet circulated by FDP activists in McComb urging blacks to refuse to fight in Vietnam. The incident further isolated FDP from the mainstream of the national Democratic Party. New York *Times,* August 4, 1965.

67. The most important figure in the early negotiations between the White House and Mississippi white moderates was Doug Wynn. A personal friend of Lyndon Johnson (the President was godfather to the Wynns' daughter), Wynn was Johnson's Mississippi campaign manager in 1964. In the months that followed, Wynn directed a steady stream of correspondence to Vice-President Humphrey and to presidential assistant Marvin Watson. In these letters and reports Wynn attacked FDP, the Delta Ministry, and the Child Development Group of Mississippi. At the same time, he reported to Watson that "I have gotten together a group which fairly represents current leadership among the loyal Democrats, and

believe that we can really go places with this group, provided we are given a little assistance." Wynn to Watson, November 29, 1965, Johnson Library.

68. Douglas Wynn to Hubert Humphrey, November 29, 1965, Johnson Library.

Notes to FEDERAL LAW AND THE COURTS IN THE CIVIL RIGHTS MOVEMENT
by Charles V. Hamilton

1. David E. Apter, *The Politics of Modernization* (Chicago: University of Chicago Press, 1965), p. 28.

2. *Ibid.*, p. 29.

3. *Guinn* v. *U.S.* 238 U.S. 347 (1915).

4. *Smith* v. *Allwright*, 321 U.S. 649 (1944).

5. Charles V. Hamilton, *The Bench and the Ballot: Southern Federal Judges and Black Voters* (New York: Oxford University Press, 1973).

6. See Monnet, "The Latest Phase of Negro Disfranchisement," 26 *Harvard Law Review* 42 (1912); and C. Vann Woodward, *Origins of the New South, 1877–1913* (Baton Rouge, Louisiana: Louisiana State University Press, 1951).

7. 238 U.S. 364.

8. 174 Fed. 2d. 394.

9. V. O. Key, Jr., *Southern Politics in State and Nation* (New York: Knopf, 1949), p. 576.

10. Reported in Hamilton, *Bench and the Ballot,* p. 130.

11. Genna Rae McNeil, *Groudwork, Charles Hamilton Houston and the Struggle for Civil Rights* (Philadelphia: University of Pennsylvania Press, 1983), pp. 217–218.

12. See: A. Leon Higginbotham, Jr., *In the Matter of Color, Race and the American Legal Process: The Colonial Period* (New York: Oxford University Press, 1978).

13. McNeil, *Groundwork*, p. 219.

14. Charles Warren, *The Supreme Court in United States History* (Boston: Little, Brown, 1926) vol. 1, p. 2.

15. Oliver Wendell Holmes, *The Common Law* (Boston: Little, Brown, 1881), p. 1.

16. This concept is discussed fully in C. Herman Pritchett, *The American Constitution* (New York: McGraw-Hill, 1959), pp. 46–48.

17. See: Charles V. Hamilton, *Minority Politics in Black Belt Alabama* (Eagleton Institute, 1962) on efforts of the Tuskegee Civic Association to get a congressional voting rights bill passed in the late 1950s.

18. Martin Luther King, Jr., *Stride Toward Freedom* (New York: Harper & Row, 1964), pp. 131–132.

19. Burke Marshall, *Federalism and Civil Rights* (New York: Columbia University Press, 1964), pp. 3–4.

20. *Ibid.*, pp. 49–50.

21. 388 U.S. 307 (1967).

22. 393 U.S. 175 (1968).

23. 394 U.S. 147 (1969).

24. Seymour Martin Lipset, *Political Man, the Social Bases of Politics* (1959; New York: Anchor Books, 1963), p. 64.

25. Morris B. Abram, "What Constitutes a Civil Right?" *The New York Times Magazine,* June 10, 1984.

26. Apter, *The Politics of Modernization,* pp. 33–36.

Notes to COMMENTARY

1. See, e.g., Shapiro, "Fathers and Sons: The Court, The Commentators, and the Search for Values," in Vince Blasi, ed., *The Burger Court: The Counterrevolution That Wasn't* (New Haven: Yale University Press, 1983), pp. 218–38.

2. Except of course in the definitional sense that because segregation was an institution sustained in various ways by law, its elimination would in that sense have to involve the law as well.

3. I acknowledge that this overview washes out many important details, but I believe that it captures the general outlines of the appropriate comparisons.

4. To finesse the issue of affirmative action, I could describe these as rules that draw lines on the basis of black-ness.

5. Analytically, this is a subcategory of the second category, because it could be described as the enforcement of a rule that the government will let anyone do whatever he or she wants. As a matter of constitutional doctrine, the state action requirement involves this category of governmental action, as does part of the law of federalism, which leaves it to the states to decide whether or not to stand aside.

6. This categorization should indicate why I am uncomfortable with Professor Hamilton's suggestion that we should sharply distinguish between claims to rights and claims to resources. In my view, claims to resources are simply challenges to governmental decisions to act in the third way, and demands that it act in the fourth.

7. *Brown v. Board of Education,* 354 U.S. 483 (1954); *Gomillion v. Lightfoot,* 364 U.S. 339 (1960).

8. *Strauder v. West Virginia,* 100 U.S. 303 (1880); *Yick Wo v. Hopkins,* 118 U.S. 356 (1886).

9. Of course the Court had not repudiated its 1896 decision in *Plessy v. Ferguson,* 163 U.S. 537 (1896). But after 1920 it had not endorsed that decision either. This is not to say that one would have expected the Court to overturn *Plessy* had the issue been presented to it in 1925; I mean to suggest only that the doctrinal structure of constitutional law was well-established, with respect to this category of action, well before the civil rights movement of the 1950s began to place pressure on the governing coalition.

10. *Lassiter v. Northampton County,* 360 U.S. 45 (1959); *Harper v. Virginia Board,* 383 U.S. 663 (1966).

11. *Smith v. Allwright,* 321 U.S. 649 (1944); *Shelley v. Kraemer,* 334 U.S. 1 (1948).

12. *Burton v. Wilmington Parking Authority,* 365 U.S. 715 (1961); *Barrows v. Jackson,* 346 U.S. 249 (1953).

13. Of course the courts had to, and did, subsequently interpret these statutes in ways that made them rather potent, at least for a while. But Congress took the initiative in the matter, after which the courts, once again acting as part of the governing coalition, cooperated to make the new policy effective.

14. See *Guinn v. U.S.,* 238 U.S. 347 (1915).

15. I say this because, to the extent that the cases raised issues that were important to some elements of the governing coalition—Southern Democrats

who were part of the New Deal coalition—they made it difficult for the courts, as another part of the coalition, to act against their (sometime) partners.

16. Even in Virginia, the effects of the invalidation of the white primary were quite limited. See Andrew Buni, *The Negro in Virginia Politics, 1902–1965* (Charlottesville: University Press of Virginia, 1967). On the white primary cases generally, see Darlene Clark Hine, *Black Victory: The Rise and Fall of the White Primary* (Millwood, NY: KTO Press, 1979).

17. See, e.g., *Jones v. Alfred H. Mayer Co.*, 392 U.S. 409 (1968).

18. See Steven F. Lawson, *Black Ballots: Voting Rights in the South, 1944–1969* (New York: Columbia University Press, 1976).

19. Monrad Paulsen, "The Sit-In Cases of 1964: 'But Answer Came There None,'" 1964 *Supreme Court Review* 137.

20. See Bernard Schwartz, *The Unpublished Opinions of the Warren Court* (New York: Oxford University Press, 1985), at pp. 143–90.

21. See *Hamm v. City of Rock Hill*, 379 U.S. 306 (1964).

22. It should be noted that the Court did nothing about discrimination in employment until Congress gave it the Civil Rights Act of 1964 to interpret and enforce.

23. See Charles S. Bullock, III, and Harrell R. Rodgers, Jr., *Law and Social Change: Civil Rights Laws and Their Consequences* (New York: McGraw-Hill, 1972).

24. *Kastzenbach v. McClung*, 379 U.S. 294 (1964); *Heart of Atlanta Motel v. United States*, 379 U.S. 241 (1964).

25. *Katzenbach v. Morgan*, 384 U.S. 641 (1966).

26. Certainly purely political considerations played the primary role in determining the Administration's response to the civil rights movement. Yet the fact that concepts of federalism were in the process of change meant that advocates of a more forceful role for the national government could not demonstrate that their positions were consistent with the law of federalism, and that those who opposed a more forceful role, even if their opposition was grounded in political calculation, could plausibly argue that doing more than they were doing would be incompatible with fundamental constitutional norms.

27. See generally David P. Currie, "The Three-Judge District Court in Constitutional Litigation," *University of Chicago Law Review*, 32 (Autumn 1964), pp. 1–79.

28. See, e.g. *Dombrowski v. Pfister*, 380 U.S. 479 (1965).

29. Compare *City of Greenwood v. Peacock*, 384 U.S. 808 (1966), *Georgia v. Rachel*, 384 U.S. 780 (1966).

Notes to THE END OF ONE STRUGGLE, THE BEGINNING OF ANOTHER
by William H. Chafe

1. Vincent Harding's remarks come from a film of Ella Baker's life—entitled FUNDI—which was produced by Joanne Grant in 1981.

2. The history of the black community in Greensboro during the civil rights era can be found in William H. Chafe, *Civilities and Civil Rights: Greensboro, North Carolina and the Black Struggle for Freedom* (New York: Oxford University Press, 1980).

3. The Mississippi movement is described in Howell Raines, *My Soul Is*

Rested: Movement Days in the Deep South Remembered (New York: G.P. Putnam, 1977); James Forman, *The Making of Black Revolutionaries* (New York: Macmillan, 1972); and numerous other works by such participants as Anne Moody, Elizabeth Sutherland, and Bernice Reagon. See also forthcoming works by John Dittmer and a new film on the life of Fannie Lou Hamer. I am also indebted to a former student, Joseph Sinsheimer, for his reports on the Mississippi movement based on conversations with Ed King and Robert Moses.

4. For an example of the conservative argument see Terry Eastland and William J. Bennett, *Counting By Race: Equality from the Founding Fathers to Bakke and Weber* (New York: Basic, 1979) Nathan Glazer's *Affirmative Discrimination: Ethnic Inequality as Public Policy* (New York: Harper and Row, 1976) makes a similar case.

5. On the SNCC experience see Forman, *The Making of Black Revolutionaries*, and Clayborne Carson, *In Struggle: SNCC and the Black Awakening of the 1960s* (Cambridge: Harvard University Press, 1981). See also Howard Zinn's classic work, *SNCC: The New Abolitionists* (Boston: Beacon, 1965).

6. Rustin's call for a domestic Marshall Plan appeared in numerous publications and his general stance is summarized in his "Protest and Politics" article in *Commentary* in April 1965. For descriptions of Johnson's commitment, see Doris Kearns, *Lyndon Johnson and the American Dream* (New York: Harper and Row, 1976). The material on Kennedy is based on research into his stance on the antipoverty question in the Kennedy Papers of the John F. Kennedy Library.

7. On the war on poverty, see James L. Sundquist, *Politics and Policy: The Eisenhower, Kennedy, and Johnson Years* (Washington, D.C.: Brookings, 1968); Sundquist, ed., *On Fighting Poverty: Perspectives from Experience* (New York: Basic, 1969); Daniel Moynihan, *Maximum Feasible Misunderstanding: Community Action in the War on Poverty* (New York: Free Press, 1969); and James T. Patterson, *America's Struggle Against Poverty, 1900–1980* (Cambridge: Harvard University Press, 1981). See also, Allen J. Matusow, *The Unraveling of America: A History of Liberalism in the 1960s* (New York: Harper and Row, 1984).

8. Forman and Carson are the best sources for an understanding of how the Black Power movement evolved.

9. On the evolution of King's thought, see David L. Lewis, *King: A Critical Biography* (New York: Praeger, 1970); Stephen B. Oates, *Let the Trumpet Sound: The Life of Martin Luther King, Jr.* (New York: Harper and Row, 1982); and Vincent Harding's essay on King in Michael V. Namorato, ed., *Have We Overcome? Race Relations Since Brown* (Jackson: University Press of Mississippi, 1981). On Kennedy, see Arthur M. Schlesinger, Jr., *Robert Kennedy and His Times* (Boston: Houghton Mifflin, 1976), and Jack Newfield, *Robert F. Kennedy: A Memoir* (New York: Dutton, 1969).

10. On the politics of the 1970s, see Kevin Phillips, *The Emerging Republican Majority* (New Rochelle: Arlington House, 1969); Rowland Evans and Robert Novak, *Nixon in the White House: The Frustration of Power* (New York: Random House, 1972); and Jonathan Schell, *The Time of Illusion* (New York: Knopf, 1976). See also Everett Ladd, Jr., *Transformation of the American Party System: Political Coalitions from the New Deal to the 1970s* (New York: Norton, 1975). On the impact of counter-intelligence operations, see David J. Garrow, *The FBI and Martin Luther King, Jr.* (New York: Norton, 1981), as well as the Senate Intelligence Committee's published hearings on the use of agents provocateur. I have also had access to FOIPA materials on the use of infiltration and provocation.

11. On the contemporary women's movement, see Sara Evans, *Personal Politics:*

The Roots of Women's Liberation in the Civil Rights Movement and the New Left (New York: Knopf, 1979), and Jo Freeman, *The Politics of Women's Liberation: A Case Study of an Emerging Social Movement and Its Relation to the Policy Process* (New York: McKay, 1975).

12. Much of this data is summarized in William J. Wilson, *The Declining Significance of Race: Blacks and Changing American Institutions* (Chicago: University of Chicago Press, 1978). See also, Jacqueline Jones, *Labor of Love, Labor of Sorrow: Black Women, Work, and the Family from Slavery to the Present* (New York: Basic, 1985).

13. Wilson, *Declining Significance of Race*.

14. See Jones, *Labor of Love, Labor of Sorrow*, and Barbara Ehrenreich, "Le Nouveau Poor," *Ms.* (July–August 1982). See also Mary Rubin, *Women and Poverty* (Research Summary Series Number 4, National Business and Professional Women's Foundation, Washington, D.C., 1982).

15. The statistics are from Kenneth Auletta, *The Underclass* (New York: Random House, 1982).

Bibliographical Essay

Scholarly study of the Civil Rights Movement has just begun. In the last decade the first studies of many important topics have appeared, and in the coming years many more will extend and revise our knowledge and understanding of the movement. In addition, participants in and observers of the movement have recorded their own memoirs and recollections of their momentous experiences. The works cited below should serve only as an introduction to the growing literature on the Civil Rights Movement.

Two adequate surveys of the Civil Rights Movement are Harvard Sitkoff's *The Struggle for Black Equality, 1954–1980* (New York: Hill and Wang, 1981), and Rhoda Lois Blumberg's *Civil Rights: The 1960s Freedom Struggle* (Boston: Twayne, 1984). Anthony L. Lewis provides a useful account through the early 1960s in *Portrait of a Decade: The Second American Revolution* (New York: Random House, 1964), and *The Origins of the Civil Rights Movement: Black Communities Organizing for Change* (New York: Free Press, 1984) by the sociologist Aldon D. Morris similarly stops in 1963. Pulitzer Prize-winning journalist Harry S. Ashmore gives a more personal analysis in *Hearts and Minds: The Anatomy of Racism from Roosevelt to Reagan* (New York: McGraw-Hill, 1982).

Background to the movement of the 1950s and 1960s can be obtained from C. Vann Woodward's sweeping, interpretative *The Strange Career of Jim Crow* (1955; 3rd rev. ed., New York: Oxford University Press, 1974) and the early chapters in Richard Kluger's impressive *Simple Justice: The History of Brown v. Board of Education and Black America's Struggle for Equality* (New York: Knopf, 1976). Two other standard works provide the context of southern and black history: George Brown Tindall, *The Emergence of the New South, 1913–1945* (Baton Rouge: Louisiana State University Press, 1967), and John Hope Franklin, *From Slavery to Freedom: A History of Negro Americans* (New York: Knopf, 1947, and later editions). Important monographs on the early period include Harvard Sitkoff, *A New Deal for Blacks; The Emergence of Civil Rights as a National Issue: The Depression Decade* (New York: Oxford University Press, 1978), Nancy J. Weiss, *Farewell to the Party of Lincoln:*

Black Politics in the Age of FDR (Princeton: Princeton University Press, 1983), Herbert Garfinkel, *When Negroes March: The March on Washington Movement in the Organizational Politics for FEPC* (New York: Free Press, 1959), Richard M. Dalfiume, *Desegregation of the U.S. Armed Forces: Fighting on Two Fronts, 1939–1953* (Columbia: University of Missouri Press, 1969), and Donald McCoy and Richard T. Reutten, *Quest and Response: Minority Rights and the Truman Administration* (Lawrence: University of Kansas Press, 1973). Essays from an earlier symposium in Robert Haws, ed., *The Age of Segregation: Race Relations in the South, 1890–1945* (Jackson: University Press of Mississippi, 1978) are also helpful.

Biographies of several important leaders in the Civil Rights Movement are among the essays in John Hope Franklin and August Meier, eds., *Black Leaders of the Twentieth Century* (Urbana: University of Illinois Press, 1982); included are Charles H. Houston, Adam Clayton Powell, Jr., Martin Luther King, Jr., Malcolm X, and Whitney M. Young, Jr. The best biography of Martin Luther King, Jr., is still David L. Lewis's *King: A Biography* (Urbana: University of Illinois Press, 1978; originally published in 1970 as *King: A Critical Biography*), but see also Stephen B. Oates, *Let the Trumpet Sound: The Life of Martin Luther King, Jr.* (New York: Harper and Row, 1982) and David J. Garrow's forthcoming *Bearing the Cross: Martin Luther King, Jr., and the Southern Christian Leadership Conference, 1955–1968.* For King's own writings see James M. Washington, ed., *A Testament of Hope: The Essential Writings of Martin Luther King., Jr.* (New York: Harper and Row, 1986). Though many important individuals have not yet been studied, other noteworthy biographies include Genna Rae McNeil, *Groundwork: Charles Hamilton Houston and the Struggle for Civil Rights* (Philadelphia: University of Pennsylvania Press, 1983), and Peter Goldman, *The Death and Life of Malcolm X* (1973; rev. 2nd ed., Urbana: University of Illinois Press, 1979). Among the numerous autobiographical accounts, see, for examples, *Standing Fast: The Autobiography of Roy Wilkins* (New York: Viking, 1982) by the long-time leader of the NAACP; *Lay Bare the Heart: An Autobiography of the Civil Rights Movement* (New York: Arbor House, 1985) by James Farmer of CORE; Cleveland Sellers, *The River of No Return: The Autobiography of a Black Militant and the Life and Death of SNCC* (New York: Morrow, 1973); and the classic by Ann Moody, *Coming of Age in Mississippi* (New York: Dell, 1968). Howell Raines skillfully collected the recollections of more than fifty participants in *My Soul Is Rested: Movement Days in the Deep South Remembered* (New York: Putnam, 1977).

Two major civil rights organizations have received exemplary treatment in August Meier and Elliott M. Rudwick, CORE: A Study in the Civil Rights Movement, 1942–1968 (New York: Oxford University Press, 1973), and Clayborne Carson, In Struggle: SNCC and the Black Awakening of the 1960s (Cambridge: Harvard University Press, 1981). No similar studies exist for the NAACP, the Urban League, or the Southern Christian Leadership Conference, but for the earlier years see Nancy J. Weiss, The National Urban League, 1910–1940 (New York: Oxford University Press, 1974), and B. Joyce Ross, J. E. Spingarn and the Rise of the NAACP, 1911–1939 (New York: Atheneum, 1972).

The courts and school desegregation have received considerable scholarly attention. Richard Kluger's previously cited Simple Justice tells in wonderful detail the story of the original 1954 cases, while Benjamin Muse, Ten Years of Prelude: The Story of Integration Since the Supreme Court's 1954 Decision (New York: Viking, 1964) and Reed Sarratt, The Ordeal of Desegregation: The First Decade (New York: Harper and Row, 1968) trace the course of implementation of Brown. Tony Freyer stresses the importance of court action in The Little Rock Crisis: A Constitutional Interpretation (Westport: Greenwood, 1985). In From Brown to Bakke: The Supreme Court and School Integration, 1954–1978 (New York: Oxford University Press, 1979), J. Harvie Wilkinson III charts the tortuous course the high court followed after Brown. Two works have been highly critical of the court's handling of school segregation; see the controversial works by a professor of constitutional law, Lino A. Graglia's Disaster by Decree: The Supreme Court Decisions on Race and the Schools (Ithaca: Cornell University Press, 1976), and by a historian, Raymond Wolters's The Burden of Brown: Thirty Years of School Desegregation (Knoxville: University of Tennessee Press, 1984). A more general work is Loren Miller, The Petitioners: The Story of the Supreme Court of the United States and the Negro (New York: Pantheon, 1966), and a study specifically on the important Fifth Circuit Court of Appeals is Jack Bass, Unlikely Heroes (New York: Simon and Schuster, 1981).

The political ramifications of the Civil Rights Movement have been analyzed in a variety of ways. The Eisenhower and Kennedy administration have been assessed by Robert F. Burk, The Eisenhower Administration and Black Civil Rights (Knoxville: University of Tennessee Press, 1984), and Carl M. Brauer, John F. Kennedy and the Second Reconstruction (New York: Columbia University Press, 1977). David J. Garrow uncovers the FBI's interest in Martin Luther King, Jr., in The FBI and Martin Luther King, Jr.: From "Solo" to Memphis (New York: Norton, 1981). Two books by Steven F. Lawson have examined the quest for the vote by blacks and then the results of their voting in *Black Ballots: Voting Rights in the South, 1944–1969* (New York: Columbia University Press, 1976) and *In Pursuit of Power: Southern Blacks and Electoral Politics, 1965–1982* (New York: Columbia University Press, 1985); a similar account by journalists is Pat Watters and Reese Cleghorn's *Climbing Jacob's Ladder: The Arrival of Negroes in Southern Politics* (New York: Harcourt, Brace and World, 1967). Sociologist Doug McAdam stresses the essentially local and political nature of the movement in his *Political Process and the Development of Black Insurgency, 1930–1970* (Chicago: University of Chicago Press, 1982). The effects of the civil rights movement on southern politics are discussed in Numan V. Bartley and Hugh David Graham, *Southern Politics and the Second Reconstruction* (Baltimore: The Johns Hopkins University Press, 1975), Earl Black, *Southern Governors and Civil Rights: Racial Segregation as a Campaign Issue in the Second Reconstruction* (Cambridge: Harvard University Press, 1976), and Alexander P. Lamis, *The Two-Party South* (New York: Oxford University Press, 1984).

Southern resistance to the Civil Rights Movement, especially to desegregation, has been studied by Numan V. Bartley, *The Rise of Massive Resistance: Race and Politics in the South During the 1950's* (Baton Rouge: Louisiana State University Press, 1969), Neil R. McMillen, *The Citizens' Council: Organized Resistance to the Second Reconstruction, 1954–1964* (Urbana: University of Illinois Press, 1971), and James W. Ely, Jr., *The Crisis of Conservative Virginia: The Byrd Organization and the Politics of Massive Resistance* (Knoxville: University of Tennessee Press, 1976). The responses of businessmen in fourteen cities are analyzed in Elizabeth Jacoway and David R. Colburn, eds., *Southern Businessmen and Desegregation* (Baton Rouge: Louisiana State University Press, 1982), but few other works deal with the reactions of white southerners who were not hard-line segregationists; for an exception see Hugh Davis Graham, *Crisis in Print: Desegregation and the Press in Tennessee* (Nashville: Vanderbilt University Press, 1967), which is broader than the title indicates.

The movement at the important local, community level has been explored in three significant works. William H. Chafe studies the site of the first sit-ins in *Civilities and Civil Rights: Greensboro, North Carolina, and the Black Struggle for Freedom* (New York: Oxford University Press, 1980). David R. Colburn has probed the history of race relations in one city in *Racial Change and Community Crisis: St. Augustine, Florida, 1877–1980* (New York: Columbia University Press, 1985). In perhaps the best local study yet, Robert J. Norrell examines one Alabama community in *Reaping the Whirlwind: The Civil Rights Movement in Tuskegee* (New York: Knopf, 1985).

In addition to the many important local communities that have not been studied, other aspects of the Civil Rights Movement have yet to receive scholarly attention. Except for Sara Evans's *Personal Politics: The Roots of Women's Liberation in the Civil Rights Movement and the New Left* (New York: Knopf, 1979), no work has examined the contribution of women, either collectively or individually through biographies of Coretta Scott King, Ella Baker, and others. Little significant work has been published on the role of the churches, black and white, or of religion generally in the movement, though many recognize their importance. David J. Garrow considers the way the national news media handled events in Selma in his *Protest at Selma: Martin Luther King, Jr., and the Voting Rights Act of 1965* (New Haven: Yale University Press, 1979), but no other studies have appeared on the way television, magazines, and national newspapers covered the movement. No scholar has analyzed the literature and music of the movement itself or later fictional treatments of it. Much work remains to be done.

Finally, three document collections provide easy access to the original words of the people involved in the movement: Albert P. Blaustein and Robert L. Zangrando, eds., *Civil Rights and the American Negro: A Documentary History* (New York: Trident, 1968), August Meier, Elliott Rudwick, and Francis L. Broderick, eds., *Black Protest Thought in the Twentieth Century* (New York: Bobbs-Merril, 1971), and Richard A. Bardolph, ed., *The Civil Rights Record: Black Americans and the Law, 1844–1970* (New York: Crowell, 1970).

Contributors

Clayborne Carson is associate professor of history at Stanford University and the author of *In Struggle: SNCC and the Black Awakening of the 1960s*. He is editor of the papers of Martin Luther King, Jr.

William H. Chafe is professor of history at Duke University and co-director of its Oral History Program. His books include *Civilities and Civil Rights: Greensboro, North Carolina, and the Black Struggle for Freedon* and *The Unfinished Journey: America Since World War II*.

John Dittmer is chairman of the department of history at DePauw University. His first book was *Black Georgia in the Progressive Era, 1900–1920*.

David J. Garrow is associate professor of political science at the City College of New York. He has written *Protest at Selma: Martin Luther King, Jr., and the Voting Rights Act of 1965* and *The FBI and Martin Luther King, Jr.: From "Solo" to Memphis*.

Charles V. Hamilton is Wallace S. Sayre Professor of Government at Columbia University. His publications include *Black Power* (with Stokely Carmichael) and *The Bench and the Ballot: Southern Federal Judges and Black Voters*.

Steven F. Lawson is associate professor of history at the University of South Florida and the author of *Black Ballots: Voting Rights in the South, 1944–1969* and *In Pursuit of Power: Southern Blacks and Electoral Politics, 1965–1982*.

David Levering Lewis is Martin Luther King, Jr., Professor of History at Rutgers University. His books include *King: A Critical Biography* and *When Harlem Was in Vogue*.

Neil R. McMillen is professor of history at the University of Southern Mississippi and has written *The Citizens' Council: Organized Resistance to the Second Reconstruction*.

J. Mills Thornton, III, is professor of history at the University of Michigan and the author of *Politics and Power in a Slave Society: Alabama, 1800–1860*.

Mark V. Tushnet is professor of law at the Georgetown University Law

Center, and is the author of *The American Law of Slavery, 1810–1860: Considerations of Humanity and Interest.*

Nancy J. Weiss is professor of history and Master of Dean Mathey College at Princeton University. Her publications include *The National Urban League, 1910–1940* and *Farewell to the Party of Lincoln: Black Politics in the Age of FDR.*

Index